FROM THE REPUBLIC OF CONSCIENCE

AN INTERNATIONAL ANTHOLOGY OF POETRY

EDITED BY

KERRY FLATTLEY &

CHRIS WALLACE-CRABBE

WHITE PINE PRESS
in association with
AMNESTY INTERNATIONAL

This edition has been wholly made up and printed in Australia
for release in the United States of America by White Pine Press
and in Australia by Aird Books Pty Ltd.

Aird Books Pty Ltd   White Pine Press
PO Box 122   76 Center Street
Flemington   Fredonia
Victoria, 3031   New York 14063
Australia   USA

First published by Aird Books in 1992
Released in the USA by White Pine Press in 1993
ISBN 1-877727-26-1

The publication and distribution of this book in the United States
was made possible, in part, by a grant from the National
Endowment for the Arts.

Consulting publisher: Jackie Yowell, Aird Books
Designer: Helen Semmler
Typeset in Baskerville by Aird Books and Asset Type, Melbourne
Printed in Australia by Australian Print Group, Maryborough, Victoria

Contents

III *It takes much time to kill a tree*

IV *Last night . . . I disappeared*

V *Darkness begets itself*   99

VI *Woman of earth, woman of fire*   129

Acknowledgements

Amnesty International, the editors and the publishers express their gratitude to the poets, or other copyright-holders, who generously gave permission for the use of their poems at no fee so that this anthology would be possible. Royalties on this book, and profits from sales of it through Amnesty offices, shall go to Amnesty International to support their work worldwide. (Details of copyright-holders are given in the Source acknowledgements at the end of this book.)

Thanks also go to the many people who have given encouragement and support to the project of this anthology, particularly: Catholic Ladies' College, Eltham, for generous use of resources and facilities; the Australian Centre, Melbourne, whose fax also ran hot; Lucy Sussex of the Department of English, University of Melbourne, for her research assistance; and Jenny Mitchell, Coordinator, Amnesty International (Victorian Branch).

Editors' notes

As this anthology was being compiled, in 1991-92, the world map changed. Countries that existed last year disappeared and some are still in the process of being redrawn and named as we go to press. We have therefore retained the names of countries as they were when we selected the poems – for example, USSR, Yugoslavia.

In reprinting poems, we have retained the style – e.g., the Australian, British or American variations of English spelling – as submitted, in respect for the variety of cultural traditions represented.

SA'DI YUSUF (*Lebanon*)

Hamra Night

A candle in a long street
A candle in the sleep of houses
A candle for frightened shops
A candle for bakeries
A candle for a journalist trembling in an empty office
A candle for a fighter
A candle for a woman doctor watching over patients
A candle for the wounded
A candle for plain talk
A candle for the stairs
A candle for a hotel packed with refugees
A candle for a singer
A candle for broadcasters in their hideouts
A candle for a bottle of water
A candle for the air
A candle for two lovers in a naked flat
A candle for the falling sky
A candle for the beginning
A candle for the ending
A candle for the last communiqué
A candle for conscience
A candle in my hands.

Translated by Abdullah al-Udhari

Introduction

During the Stalinist Terror, Anna Akhmatova queued for seventeen months outside the prisons of Leningrad. Together with thousands of others, she waited to hand in a parcel, or gain some news of a loved one. She wrote of the following exchange:

Beside me, in the queue, there was a woman with blue lips. She had, of course, never heard of me; but she suddenly came out of that trance so common to us all and whispered in my ear (everybody spoke in whispers there): "Can you describe this?" And I said: "Yes, I can." And then something like the shadow of a smile crossed what had once been her face.

What did the woman want described? And what was it about the poet's reply that brought to her the flicker of hope? We may be sure that the woman was not asking the poet to do something she could have done for herself. What she wanted described was much more than the length of the queues or the freezing temperatures, and it went beyond the all-pervading brutality and despair. What she wanted was out of her own reach, and we can sense the desperate nature of her plea. It had to do with who she was, with who everyone was, with what was happening. She wanted her world named and she wanted herself named, much the same as, some fifty years later, Irina Ratushinskaya would say, "Give me a name, prison". This was where the woman's hope lay: in the desperate conviction that as long as there were those who could name the darkness, then all was not lost. In the poet's reply and in the flicker of the woman's smile, we sense a realignment of forces, a shift in the foundations beneath the structures of power.

To understand the woman's question and the poet's reply is to understand the importance of this anthology. The woman's question is ours – asked of our time. We ask of this century: can someone describe it, name it, for us? Can the dimensions of a horror that has seen us, outside war, kill well over fifty million of our own kind be given shape in words? The poets answer "yes" to this question.

>   But play, you must,
> A tune beyond us, yet ourselves,
> A tune upon the blue guitar
> Of things exactly as they are.
>   (WALLACE STEVENS)

It is this "things exactly as they are" that is the poets' business. This location is their habitation. That is where the poetry is. Even in a secular time, the language of poetry is in some sense sacred. It is this fundamental difference between the poet's language and all other language that gives poetry its uniqueness: its authority in times of despair and hopelessness.

Poetry does not depict a world that can be measured or described by political analysis and expert commentary. It is not news. Rather it names the particular shape of our humanity, still dressed in the garb of everyday experience, but made extraordinary, because clearly seen, perhaps for the first time. Our lives are always slipping away from us, but sometimes they are brutally and violently taken. Poetry gives them back, no matter how disfigured they might be. And because it gives them back it trumps the hand of the controllers – the ideologues, the propagandists, the dissemblers, the censors, the gaolers, the torturers, and all the fanatics of order.

> Poetry
> When she comes
> 　　　　respects nothing
> 　　　　(FERREIRA GULLAR)

This is why it restores and redeems, and this is why the controllers quite rightly see it as the most dangerous of all enemies, much as Plato suspected it long ago. It is "serious love" (Yang Lian). It

> kisses . . .
> the eyes of those who . . .
> . . . thirst for happiness
> 　　　　and justice
> And promises to set the country on fire.
> 　　　　(FERREIRA GULLAR)

What we have sought to do in this selection is allow poetry to bear witness to the concerns that lie at the heart of Amnesty International. That Amnesty has to exist in our world at all is a continually shocking realisation. Yet, given the sickness of the world, we can only be thankful for its presence. Since its foundation in 1961 Amnesty has stood by its charter to work independently of all interest groups in the promotion and protection of human rights. Amnesty now exists in 150 countries and has over one million members. For many of these members, belonging to Amnesty is intrinsic to their own humanity, for it finds its rationale in the belief that all people are equal in dignity, and that the dignity of the individual is inseparable from that of the whole. Not to defend the dignity of another is therefore to diminish one's own. Amnesty also recognises that our humanity is not given, but must be continually chosen, cherished and protected.

We began the process of selection for this anthology by gathering poems from around the world that not only addressed the concerns of Amnesty about human rights abuses, but included those that explored the moral landscape of our time – not just the outer terrain, but also the inner. We allowed the poems to fall into groups, seven in all, beginning with the place of poetry and ending with poems of hope. Within each part, the poems are arranged not only to speak to us but also to each other.

It was Anna Akhmatova who asked, "Why is our century worse than any other?" It is difficult for us to imagine a worse century. But do we mean in degree, or in kind? Is it simply that, with increasingly sophisticated means, we can kill, maim and suppress more efficiently and on a grander scale? Or has something new been unleashed, perhaps always there, waiting in the blood like a fatal virus? The poets lead us to suspect something new. They open the door to our dwelling and take us in to look around, and we become aware of a prevailing mood that permeates even the timbers and fabrics. In a phrase, this mood is an absence of trust in our own humanity. Our age has disposed of the old myths but the new myths have been unable to contain us:

We dreamed, woke, doubted, wept for fading stars
And then projected brave new avatars,
 Triumphs of reason. Yet a whole dimension
 Had vanished from the chambers of the mind . . .
    (CHRIS WALLACE-CRABBE)

A vanished dimension, yes. But not a vanished yearning. A yearning for something big enough to contain our paradoxes and contradictions. Big enough to save us:

And yet there must exist
a zone of salvation . . .
dull are the people who have no outlet from themselves . . .
    (NINA CASSIAN)

Yet the human desire for transcendence is often thought of today as an unfortunate aberration, and people have a deep suspicion of salvation.

   He does not dare look out the window,
for the third rail, the unbroken draught of poison,
runs there beside him. He regards it as a disease
he has inherited the susceptibility to. He has to keep
his hands in his pockets, as others must wear mufflers.
    (ELIZABETH BISHOP)

We keep our hands in our pockets, and, unable to say "yes" to ourselves, we lack a "no" that is sure enough to stand between our best and our worst interests. We are left to make do with plans and policies that have little bearing on the main plot. It is a different play that is being staged, and we are actors and audience both, but unable to change the script.

It is this sense of helplessness that pervades so many of the poems about our time. That there is a great conflict being waged, we have no doubt, and we are also certain that it has something to do with ourselves. Yet we don't think of ourselves as participants, as having any influence on the outcome. Believing ourselves to be ineffectual we remain passive, benumbed. The dimensions, and even the nature of the conflict are beyond us. Apprehensively, we wait. Words and speech are unable to convey any sense of what is happening (Akhmatova: "And we don't want to talk"; Pilinszky: "I do not understand the human speech"). We hibernate (Sorescu: "Every year life salutes us with 365 shots of sun"). We are anonymous (Fernando: "Silence is our mask"). We turn to endless distractions (Faraz: "Relax, don't think so much") and unfounded optimism (Wallace-Crabbe: "The fond cushions of our belief"). The overwhelming feeling is of a great vacuum, and into this vast space something has rushed and been unleashed. It is an age in which a high school can become a prison, a torture cell, a death chamber, and finally, a museum, in the space of a few years (Cardenal: "A Museum in Kampuchea"). Outside, there are still white geese in puddles. The sun rises and sets. The moon fills the sky at night. Yet there is a profound unease. Human beings are alone with themselves, waiting for an ending.

It is against this background that we set the central clusters of poems: clusters gathered around the themes of censorship, disappearances, aspects of horror, and the particular experience of women.

The temptation to censor is present for all those who have power. This is because power carries with it the presumption of 'knowing best'. Its tendency is therefore to consolidate itself and become its own end. This is a tendency even for the most benign of governments, but for dictatorships it is a central dynamic. Control is the obsession of the censor, and the logic of censorship is not only that different beliefs and points of view be suppressed. More profoundly, it is that the conditions in which divergent views might become possible are also suppressed. The censoring mentality therefore tries to block the wellsprings of human freedom: imagination, exploration, inquisitiveness, spontaneity:

> That thing's alive! Its dangerous. Make away
>   with it!

> (D.H. LAWRENCE)

The zeal of the censor knows no bounds. This can have a ludicrous dimension, as in the poems by Rajendra, Shigeji and Kraus. It can also be ominous, as in Patel's 'On Killing a Tree':

> It takes much time to kill a tree,
> Not a simple jab of the knife
> Will do it.
> . . .
> No,
> The root is to be pulled out . . .

There is no clear line between the decision to censor and the decision to arrest, torture and kill people for their beliefs. A censored society is an imprisoned society:

I glance down at my shoe and – there's the lace!
This can't be gaol then, can it, in that case.
(GYÖRGY PETRI)

However, the ideologues and bully-boys reserve a special vehemence for those who are behind prison walls because of their beliefs. These people represent something far more dangerous than the common criminal. Their very difference is an affront, because it challenges the fantasy that the world could be a simple, predictable, controllable and uniform place. The political prisoner therefore becomes the embodiment of all that must be eradicated; no longer a human being, but another species to which a different set of criteria apply:

"Things like these
I have no time for;

they are worse than rats;
you can only shoot them."
(DENNIS BRUTUS)

Anyone whose presence challenges the authority of the regime is the most likely victim of deprivation, torture and execution:

They have him squeezed   into the square room
Patrick Shivers   stripped naked   a tight bag
covering his head   feet splayed   rope round his neck
(VINCENT BUCKLEY)

Don't tell me the political layout of your crimes;
I only stoke up furnaces for those I receive to roast
. . .
I am the guard charged with executions.
(LUPENGA MPHANDE)

Of course those who do come under the watchful eye of the State may be dealt with in another way. They may become 'The Disappeared' – this strange new noun that cannot comprehend its own meaning. These people are not officially arrested. They are not formally imprisoned. They are not officially tortured. They are not officially killed. Nor do they cease to exist. They disappear, and as such, stay with those left behind:

if pain were only finger flesh
which can be rubbed on stone wall
so it hurt hurts visibly
painfully
with tears
(RENATA PALLOTTINI)

Grief is the growth of scar tissue. However, for those left behind, there is only the open wound.

This deliberate and calculated abuse of human sensibilities is not just a form of social control. It is also a manifestation of the more sinister dimensions of power. Power has taste buds; over time they become bored with bland fare. Mandelstam's Stalin "rolls the executions on his tongue like berries". At this extreme we dare not use the word 'human' anymore. Something else has taken its place:

> Man has ceased to be man,
> Man has become beast,
> Man has become prey.
> (DENNIS BRUTUS)

Beast and prey both. As in Judith Wright's poem:

> The will to power destroys the power to will.
> The weapon made, we cannot help but use it;
> . . .
> In the one stroke we win the world and lose it.
> The will to power destroys the power to will.

The poets do not let us dissociate ourselves from the oppressors' world. They remind us that the will to power is present in us all, and that we ignore it at our peril. Gwen Harwood's 'Barn Owl' finds it in a child, powerless in the world of adults, but "master of life and death" with an animal. Dennis Brutus asks, "who has not joyed in the arbitrary exercise of power?", and suggests that the brutal regime simply mirrors our selves.

So the ball is back in our own court. We must also deal with those dimensions in our own lives, individual or collective, which are prey to the abuse of power. Here we mention two that are relevant to Amnesty's concerns. One is the stark fact that human rights abuses, not only at the point of abuse, but also at the level of planning, appear to be an overwhelmingly male phenomenon. The other is the widespread consent that is given, within societies that consider themselves humane and civilised, to the death penalty.

In drawing attention to the prevalence of men in human rights abuses, we are not saying that the pursuit of power is merely a male characteristic. Power takes many forms, and the gender issue is too complex to resolve here. Our concern is rather with the sort of power the poets have disclosed. There can be no gainsaying the fact that it is male, most especially in its violent and its sexual forms. In the poems by Holub, Coutinho, Lavant and Pallottini, we can see the bewilderment of the mother, the wife: all too often, inheriting the empty house, the fear, and the long, muted pain that remains after the men have gone. In the poems by Brissenden, Hope and Clark (all men), we look into the simmering cauldron in which violence, hatred and fear merge with male sexuality. We are forced to ask questions about: a latent male hatred of female fecundity (Hope's 'contraceptive

6

hate'); the relationship between penetration and conquest (Clark's "Always when the conquerors come . . . it is the women who know what they say"); the relationship between violence and male sexual arousal:

> Tiretta, unbuttoned,
> Lifts from behind the long silk skirt
> Of the Pope's niece.
> The other leg comes off.
> (R.F. BRISSENDEN)

These are not questions to be afraid of, or possibilities to be ashamed of. They are issues that both men and women must explore, for the sources of our inhumanity are not just a consequence of social conditions. We carry them inside us.

The other issue that invites our scrutiny is the death penalty. Amnesty opposes the death penalty, arguing that it is a violation of the fundamental human right to life, and has no place in a humane and civilised society. In the poems by James Baxter, Thom Gunn and Stevie Smith we are confronted by the stark contrast between the barbarity of the act and the elaborate legal, social and religious procedures and proprieties with which we have disguised it. We have also included R.H. Morrison's poem, 'Black Deaths', in this group because it shows how the death penalty can still be operative in a society that no longer has it on the statutes. In our own country, Australia, a significant number of the indigenous people have hanged themselves in prison. No law allows it and no court has awarded it, but the sentence has still been carried out.

We need to ask whether support for the death penalty is a consequence of a concern for justice, or whether what makes the sentence so appealing to many people is its finality and lack of ambiguity. James Baxter's Harry Fat wants to keep the country pure, by which he actually means simple. In the face of complexity he turns to the simplicity of the trapdoor and the rope. Faced with the stirrings of mercy, he turns to the impatience of dogmatism. Could it be that it is not the criminal we want executed at all, but rather what the criminal represents – that whole confluence of weakness, failure, fear and loathing? Is the demand for capital punishment more an indication of our inability to admit our collective reality than it is a concern for justice? Perhaps also there is a secret satisfaction in retaining the power to deal our dark side such a seemingly fatal blow.

This book begins with poems about poetry; it ends with poems about hope. So the book is watched over by these two sentinels and we would not be imposing on Anna Akhmatova in paraphrasing her conversation with the woman in the Leningrad queue: '. . . she suddenly came out of that trance so common to us all and whispered in my ear . . . "Is there hope?" And I said: "Yes, there is."'

Like poetry, hope happens, and often in the most unlikely, even formidable, of circumstances. It can be present in the prison cell ('A Prison Nightfall', 'My Daughter'). It can subsist on memory ('I'll Always Remember'). It can wait in anticipation ('A Wind Will Come from the South', 'Wildstrawberry Town'). It can fly in the face of sober judgement:

> Before you go, I need to tell you . . .
> No one knows why this story is true . . .
> But I know it is not a lie.
> (PEGGY SHUMAKER)

It is, somehow, there, often in the very midst of despair, and sometimes waiting at the end. Despair, it seems, is more its companion than its enemy, sometimes co-existing, sometimes blocking out, but not necessarily forever. Indeed, in the sense that we find hope here, despair is often the crucible in which it is fired ('How Water Began to Play', 'When the Sun Shines More Years Than Fear').

Hope is also to be found in the possibility of grieving for *ourselves*, not just as we are found in this book, but also in our ordinariness. The willingness to be less than what we could be is endemic. The lack of care and the complicity of silence find us all wanting. We cannot dissociate ourselves from the hypocricies of our governments or the immoralities of our corporations. Nor can we hide behind the screen of busyness, even if we do call it 'work and family commitments'. This is classic middle-class camouflage: one of the more altruistic personae of self-interest.

It may well be that our capacity to grieve is our actual reality. Our instinctive confession of a terrible falling short may be the very grounds for hope:

> And many weep for sheer acceptance, and more
> Refuse to weep for fear of all acceptance . . .
> (LES MURRAY)

If hope does have an enemy, it is more likely to be cynicism than despair. Cynicism is the twisted face of hope, its mutant offspring. It is, of course, more fashionable, and, for many people, the only appropriate response to a world in which Amnesty is necessary. For such people, hope may well be akin to wishful thinking. However, Amnesty is not founded on wishful thinking. Like Shao Yanxiang's "weather-beaten optimism", Amnesty knows the world that it inhabits, whereas the cynic is, by very definition, one step removed. Cynicism is a disengagement, and therefore a violation, of one's humanity. The catch-cry of the cynic is 'what's the point?', which is, of course, to miss the point completely:

> The point, I imagine, is
> not to learn to expect
> betrayal, self-deceit, lies
> however thick they collect
> in the cul-de-sac of one's days . . .
> (EVAN JONES)

Hope is not a pragmatic choice. Even if Amnesty did not influence the world in any way at all, it would still have to exist if we wanted to go by the name of human.

We close with the poem that is the book's namesake, Seamus Heaney's 'From the Republic of Conscience'. It is our sincere hope that the book will sit on the shelves of that "frugal republic", that all who take it down to read will be reminded of their dual citizenship, and that they will draw courage from the sure knowledge that the republic's embassies are everywhere.

KERRY FLATTLEY
CHRIS WALLACE-CRABBE
Melbourne, 1992

I

You left me my lips, and they shape words

Willy-willy man
Winningarra.
My wild wind man
came to me one night
beside the quiet billabong
underneath a quandong tree.

ARCHIE WELLER

OSIP MANDELSTAM (*USSR*)

You took away all the oceans

You took away all the oceans and all the room.
You gave me my shoe-size in earth with bars around it.
Where did it get you? Nowhere.
You left me my lips, and they shape words, even in silence.

[VORONEZH, 1935]

Translated by Clarence Brown and W.S. Merwin

YEHUDA AMICHAI (*Israel*)

Of Three or Four in a Room

Of three or four in a room
there is always one who stands beside the window.
He must see the evil among thorns
and the fires on the hill.
And how people who went out of their houses whole
are given back in the evening like small change.
Of three or four in a room
there is always one who stands beside the window,
his dark hair above his thoughts.
Behind him, words.
And in front of him, voices wandering without a knapsack,
hearts without provisions, prophecies without water,
large stones that have been returned
and stay sealed, like letters that have no
address and no one to receive them.

Translated by Chana Bloch and Stephen Mitchell

MUHAMMAD AL-MAGHUT (*Syria*)

The Postman's Fear

Prisoners everywhere
Send me all you have
Fears screams and boredom
Fishermen of all beaches
Send me all you have
Empty nets and seasickness

Peasants of every land
Send me all you have
Flowers rags
Mutilated breasts
Ripped-up bellies
And torn-out nails
To my address . . . any café
Any street in the world
I'm preparing a *huge file*
About human suffering
To present to God
Once it's signed by the lips of the hungry
And the eyelids of those still waiting
You wretched everywhere
What I fear most is
God could be *illiterate*

.

Translated by Abdullah al-Udhari

GAO FALIN (*China*)

Flint

I am flint
I have angular edges and corners

I'm not so gorgeous as diamonds and emeralds
Nor elegant as white marble and green jade
I've never been carved into an imperial seal
That feudal lords would risk their lives to seize
Modern women don't think me worth wearing on their tender
     fingers
Or hanging around their milky necks
I can't compete with sliding glaciers and gravel
In being a heavyweight subject for geological treatises

I am flint
I make just one request
Please pick me up
– Strike

Yes   strike me very hard!
In a flash I can open like a gray cocoon
As the colorful light of life bursts from my soul's depths
Strike me and by striking prove that I
Am not mere wasted detritus even though
I've slept in a marsh or valley for ten thousand years
For I am a point of crystalized fire
Silent star
Hardened flower

Translated by Fang Dai, Dennis Ding and Edward Morin

14

YANG LIAN (*China*)

Plowing

I am a plow
I am a betrayer of cold and death
Endless fields come toward me
They carry spring's dreams
Coming toward me, the moistened moon –
My antique, exquisite body

I am grief
I hear the groans of roots being amputated
My heart is rolling and trembling
In black waves
Like a boat fighting the storm
Like a flag quietly hoisted in humiliation
I hand frozen clumps of deep earth to the sun
Making the tract claimed by loneliness and desolation
Yield a cheerful brook once again

I am serious love
I melt unlimited tenderness with an edge of steel
More sincere than an embrace and kisses
I force all wildness, poverty and hopelessness
Far away from the great land
I give my naked soul to love
Marching on forever, spreading eternal life –
Furrow upon furrow of trenches
Plot after plot of fields
Carry my longings that gradually stretch
And submerge into new green during a radiant season

Translated by Fang Dai, Dennis Ding and Edward Morin

ANNE STEVENSON (*UK*)

Making Poetry

....

"You have to inhabit poetry
if you want to make it."

And what's "to inhabit"?

To be in the habit of, to wear
words, sitting in the plainest light,
in the silk of morning, in the shoe of night;
a feeling, bare and frondish in surprising air;
familiar . . . rare.

And what's "to make"?

To be and to become words' passing
weather; to serve a girl on terrible
terms, embark on voyages over voices,
evade the ego-hill, the misery-well,
the siren hiss of *publish, success, publish,*
success, success, success.

And why inhabit, make, inherit poetry?

Oh, it's the shared comedy of the worst
blessed; the sound leading the hand;
a wordlife running from mind to mind
through the washed rooms of the simple senses;
one of those haunted, undefendable, unpoetic
crosses we have to find.

MIGUEL HUEZO MIXCO (*El Salvador*)

If Death . . .

If death should come asking for me
do me the favor
of telling him to come back tomorrow
because I still haven't paid my debts
nor finished a poem
nor said goodbye to anyone
nor prepared clothing for the trip
nor delivered that package I promised to
nor locked up my desk drawers
nor told my friends what I should have
nor sniffed the fragrance of the unborn rose
nor laid bare my roots
nor answered an overdue letter
because I haven't even washed my hands
or known a son
or gone hiking in unknown countries
nor do I know the sea's seven sails
nor the song of mariners
If death should come
please tell him I understand
and to wait a bit
because I haven't kissed my sweetheart goodbye
nor shaken hands with my family
nor dusted my books
nor whistled my favorite song
nor become reconciled with my enemies
tell him I haven't yet attempted suicide
nor seen my people freed
tell him if he comes to return tomorrow
that it's not because I fear him but because
I haven't even set off along the road.

Translated by Claribel Alegría and Darwin J. Flakoll

MONGANE WALLY SEROTE (*South Africa*)

Ofay-Watcher Looks Back

I want to look at what happened;
That done,
As silent as the roots of plants pierce the soil
I look at what happened,
Whether above the houses there is always either smoke or dust,
As there are always flies above a dead dog.
I want to look at what happened.
That done,
As silent as plants show colour: green,
I look at what happened,
When houses make me ask: do people live there?
As there is something wrong when I ask: is that man alive?
I want to look at what happened.
That done,
As silent as the life of a plant that makes you see it
I look at what happened
When knives creep in and out of people
As day and night into time.
I want to look at what happened,
That done,
As silent as plants bloom and the eye tells you:
    something has happened.
I look at what happened.
When jails are becoming necessary homes for people
Like death comes out of disease,

I want to look at what happened.

SIPHO SEPAMLA (*South Africa*)

Talk to the Peach Tree

Let's talk to the swallows visiting us in summer
ask how it is in other countries

Let's talk to the afternoon shadow
ask how the day has been so far

Let's raise our pets to our level
ask them what they don't know of us

      words have lost meaning
      like all notations they've been misused

      most people will admit
      a whining woman can overstate her case

Talk to the paralysing heat in the air
inquire how long the mercilessness will last

Let's pick out items from the rubbish heap
ask how the stench is like down there

Let's talk to the peach tree
find out how it feels to be in the ground

Let's talk to the moon going down
ask if it isn't enough eyeing what's been going on

      come on
      let's talk to the devil himself
      it's about time

OSIP MANDELSTAM (*USSR*)

Maybe this is the beginning of madness

Maybe this is the beginning of madness.
Maybe it's your conscience:
a knot of life in which we are seized and known
and untied for existence.

So in cathedrals of crystals not found on earth
the prudent spider of light
draws the ribs apart and gathers them again
into one bundle.

And gathered together by one thin beam
the bundles of pure lines give thanks.
One day they will meet, they will assemble
like guests with the visors up,

and here on earth, not in heaven,
as in a house filled with music,
if only we don't offend them, or frighten them away.
How good to live to see it!

Forgive me for what I am saying.
Read it to me quietly, quietly.

[VORONEZH, 15 MARCH 1937]

Translated by Clarence Brown and W.S. Merwin

OLGA SEDAKOVA (*USSR*)

A Chinese journey (*extract*)

10

Great
is the artist
who knows no debt
except for his debt to the brush's play
and his brush
enters into
the heart of mountains
enters into
the happiness of leaves
with one stroke
with one gentleness
rapture
confusion
with one gesture he enters into immortality
and immortality
plays
with him.
But he whom
the spirit
has deserted,
from whom the light
has been taken,
who, for the tenth time
in a troubled place
searches for the pure source,
which fell from the hand of miracles
but will not say: "These are false miracles!":
before
this person
the skies bow
submissively.

[AZAROVKA, AUGUST 1986]

Translated by Richard McKane

21

JAIME SUÁREZ QUEMAIN *(El Salvador)*

And You Again, Good Sir

....

. . . nevertheless, you, good sir,
with your respectable belly
and your profound mercantile vocation
in spite of everything
including your smile
of mangled magnolia blossoms
you, good sir, you
who not too long ago
believed in the magical power of poetry
and had dreams and observed pigeons
and played at imprisoning the sea
in an old abandoned corner . . .
you, good sir, who now speak
of the uselessness of verse and the truth
of your belly and laugh at the cartoons
and complain about Passolini, you, sir,
audacious delinquent dressed in tuxedo,
pretending to be
weathervane gargoyle,
the century's best-selling product,
when you forget the samba they're playing for
you will see the world through poetic eyes
because verse, good sir,
is also for you
it is for everybody
it wanders the streets
dawdles before shop windows
hangs from the innocent necks of children
it throbs in the blushes
of those dollies in hot pants
that you acquire at bargain prices
it climbs aboard buses
it is a friend of newsboys
and workers

and though at times
many times
it spits in your face
verse wants to redeem you
fill your gaze with smiles
inject tenderness into your veins
shelter your dreams and ward off
the nightmares that harass you
verse, good sir,
wants to change your uniform
send it off for drycleaning
and disinfect it at no charge
because even though you
elude the song of birds
you, good sir, you . . .
can still be saved.

Translated by Claribel Alegría and Darwin J. Flakoll

MAHMOUD DARWISH (*Israel/Palestine*)

I Have Witnessed the Massacre

I have witnessed the massacre
I am a victim of a map
I am the son of plain words
I have seen pebbles flying
I have seen dew drops as bombs
When they shut the gates of my heart on me
Built barricades and imposed a curfew
My heart turned into an alley
My ribs into stones
And carnations grew
And carnations grew

Translated by Abdullah al-Udhari

FERREIRA GULLAR (*Brazil*)

Subversive

....

Poetry
when she comes
              respects nothing.
Neither father nor mother.
                  When she struggles
up from one of her abysses
she ignores Society and the State
disdains Water Regulations
                hee-haws
like a young
     whore
     in front of the Palace of Dawn. *

And only later
does she reconsider: kisses
              the eyes of those who earn little
              gathers into her arms
              those who thirst for happiness
              and justice

And promises to set the country on fire.

Translated by William Jay Smith

---

* The presidential palace in Brasília

ROSALIND BRACKENBURY (*UK*)

Looking for Words

looking for words plain enough to tell the truth
looking through water for the round brown stone
I find the weight here in my palm, itself alone

touch where the word may falter
earth marked with a passing tread
grass blown flat from many partings
the wild trees' circumference

touch of wind and the sky opens
step and the rabbits leap and bounce away
glance and the heavy partridge rise before you
there is your cold hand warming
this space, this time
my fields, your foreign land

rooted here as a scarecrow
alone now, arms spread, no way
to keep the wind out or close
what is laid open
flayed by the seasons
bone upon earth I let
the winter wheat grow up between my toes
and watch the wild hares run
lit in this sun between rain clouds

looking for words plain enough to tell the truth

DUODUO (*China*)

Wake Up

Outside the window the sky is clean
inside the box thoughts sparkle

Only once in a hundred years a nod of the head
only once in a thousand years an encounter
the writing on the red brick wall is like an allegory
clean lips clean language

Quick closely closely
bring our faces together for a moment
together for a short while like this:
clean lips clean sleep

Withered leaves fall, scars turn purple
in the first place it was all one memory
we received the only favour
clean sleep clean sleep

Do not call out it will come
desire originally was a golden grain
listen to me   the only, the only thing
clean language clean language

Translated by Gregory Lee and John Cayley

MOHAN KOIRALA (*Nepal*)

My Nepali words broken, fragmented

Sugar, I write sugar, and paraffin I write,
Whether or not it is right to write poems,
But I, I write petrol queues . . .
Really whatever I write I write ink, I write poems.

Do I ask in my language whether the tempu-driver has a heart?
One should hardly write the rickshaw-driver's pedals,
    It is a poem that I write.
A motorbike I write as it chases along, music ringing,
And now I write a bus, kicking up the dust;
Perhaps a poem is not made in this way. I do not know.
    I write the flying dust.

Market prices cheap and dear, thick and thin:
The common poets talk of these. Or is it that I am one?
The great poets smile, they talk of lovely rhododendrons,
Still greater poets speak of the Himalaya,
The greatest scratch poems about Heaven and Hell,
    they can join the two together.
This is barely Nepali verse.
What are the great poets writing, their language arcane,
    their words incomprehensible?
Nobody understands at all.

Maize and millet at the mill, lined up to be ground,
With rapeseed ready for pressing,
A young queue up to the oilpress,
"Who will buy meals?
Who will buy garlic?
Who will buy ghee?"
Broken Nepali, broken lips,
"Who will buy okra?"
"Who will buy onions?"

Can Nepali poems not be written at all?

Translated by Michael Hutt

WALLACE STEVENS (*USA*)

The Man with the Blue Guitar

(*extract*)

The man bent over his guitar,
A shearsman of sorts. The day was green.

They said, "You have a blue guitar,
You do not play things as they are."

The man replied, "Things as they are
Are changed upon the blue guitar."

And they said then, "But play, you must,
A tune beyond us, yet ourselves,

A tune upon the blue guitar
Of things exactly as they are."

II

....

We can't see. But feel some awful thing

We had fed the heart on fantasies,
The heart's grown brutal from the fare;
More substance in our enmities
Than in our love . . .

W.B. YEATS

ANNA AKHMATOVA (*USSR*)

Behind the lake the moon's not stirred

Behind the lake the moon's not stirred
And seems to be a window through
Into a silent, well-lit house,
Where something unpleasant has occurred.

Has the master been brought home dead,
The mistress run off with a lover,
Or has a little girl gone missing,
And her shoes found by the creek-bed . . .

We can't see. But feel some awful thing,
And we don't want to talk.
Doleful, the cry of eagle-owls, and hot
In the garden the wind is blustering.

[1922]

Translated by D.M. Thomas

HANNES PÉTURSSON (*Iceland*)

The Crematorium in Dachau

Cunning building
of pink, slender stones,
you are not *a house*
though inhaling through doors
sunlight and sweet winds
luring from the branches
the spices of trees.

You're a starved animal
from a sunken geological age,
a starved monster
which had long dominated,
drunk blood and crunched
bones, swollen with satiety;
now prostrate on an empty belly
in the tepid gravel,
on a deflated belly,
yet not decomposed.

Translated by Sigurdur A. Magnússon

ERNESTO CARDENAL (*Nicaragua*)

A Museum in Kampuchea

....

We went into a museum that used to be a high school
but under Pol Pot the high school became
                    the biggest prison in Cambodia.
The classrooms divided into little cells.
Here one only came to die.
More than 20,000 prisoners passed through here
                    of whom only 17 survived,
the ones who hadn't yet been killed when the liberating
                                        troops arrived.
                    This was Pol Pot's 'Democratic Kampuchea'.
Here are the photos taken of them on entering.
                                They took photos of them all.
Some with their hands tied, others wearing chains
                                        and iron collars.
        The worst thing to see was the horror in their faces.
You could see they weren't looking at the camera, but at death
                    and the torture before death.
But even more shocking was a smiling face:
a girl, or teenage boy, someone innocent, unaware
evidently of what was going to happen to them.
            And photos of mothers with babies.
Some crude device for pulling out fingernails.
Tongs for tearing off nipples.
            A great many different kinds of tools . . .
The tank where they were held underwater.
The posts where they were hanged.
The cell where Pol Pot's Minister of Information was also held
                    before being killed.
More than 100 mass graves where they buried them
                                        have been found.
The infants buried with their milk bottles and pacifiers.
And the skulls, large piles of skulls
                    that nobody wants to see.
        They killed 3 of the 8 million inhabitants.
They destroyed the factories, the schools, the medicines.

They'd jail someone for wearing glasses.
       The towns remained deserted.
The whole world knew about this.
How can it be that now, since Kampuchea was liberated,
the North American press doesn't speak badly of Pol Pot?
Finally we went outside.
           There were flowers outside.
In a clean puddle a white duck fluttered
      bathing itself in the water and sun.
The young women who passed by on the street
looked like pagodas.

Translated by Jonathan Cohen

W.H. AUDEN (*UK*)

Musée des Beaux Arts

About suffering they were never wrong,
The Old Masters: how well they understood
Its human position; how it takes place
While someone else is eating or opening a window
    or just walking dully along;
How, when the aged are reverently, passionately waiting
For the miraculous birth, there always must be
Children who did not specially want it to happen, skating
On a pond at the edge of the wood:
They never forgot
That even the dreadful martyrdom must run its course
Anyhow in a corner, some untidy spot
Where the dogs go on with their doggy life and the torturer's horse
Scratches its innocent behind on a tree.

In Breughel's *Icarus*, for instance: how everything turns away
Quite leisurely from the disaster; the ploughman may
Have heard the splash, the forsaken cry,
But for him it was not an important failure; the sun shone
As it had to on the white legs disappearing into the green
Water; and the expensive delicate ship that must have seen
Something amazing, a boy falling out of the sky,
Had somewhere to get to and sailed calmly on.

[DECEMBER 1938]

Jonathan Aaron (*USA*)

Finding the Landscape

Last night you questioned the number of stars
on your index finger. Their replies were guarded,
nameless. Now, above the mist, cold planets

linger to help you interpret a message
sleep delivered in code. You read it
with your eyes closed and discover the cities

behind you are empty, the people sealed
and silent in their breathing rooms.
You stop reading and listen to a robin

sing like a drink of water. You know
there is salvation in the eye of the moment,
and coming to yourself in a tree's glitter

at half-light, you settle for it.
But the landscape is lying on its side, so you
lie down on your side to see, your assumptions

rolling from your pockets into the black acres
past the beach. Seaward, beyond anything
you expected, there are no sails, only

a glimpse of the stars you relied on shaking
into laminated darkness like fish, and the horizon
sweeping your eyes with its little white flag.

ALISON CROGGON (*Australia*)

This is the Stone

it's when you want to shrug it all off:
the gross pap of warm anaesthetised brains
hotels ringing with stale tongues
the bland translations of headlines
walls everywhere

when money's sensual brutality
chats warmly in your veins
when your possessions assert their tyranny
mocking you from corners

where is the moon's still wash
over uncluttered landscapes?
where are your lovers' mouths
which stopped your mouth so neatly?
in this dreamless city you put them away

now you turn to a window
which mimics you in ice
your face a marble of loss
your hair a curtain of dust:
this is the stone you work on

ZBIGNIEW HERBERT (*Poland*)

The Messenger

The messenger awaited a desperately long time
the longed-for herald of victory or annihilation
was delayed – the tragedy was without any ending

In the background the chorus scanned dark prophecies and curses
the king – a dynastic fish – thrashed in an inconceivable net
the second indispensable person was absent – fate

The epilogue was probably known by an eagle an oak the wind
    a sea wave
the spectators were half-dead breathing shallowly as stone
The Gods slept   A quiet night without lightning

Finally the messenger arrived in a mask of blood of dirt lamentation
uttering incomprehensible shrieks pointing with his hands
    to the East
this was worse than death because there would be no pity
    no fear at all
and in the last moment everyone longs to be pardoned

Translated by John and Bogdana Carpenter

CHRIS WALLACE-CRABBE (*Australia*)

A Wintry Manifesto

It was the death of Satan first of all,
The knowledge that earth holds though kingdoms fall,
    Inured us to a stoic resignation,
    To make the most of a shrunken neighbourhood;

And what we draw on was not gold or fire,
No cross, not cloven hoof about the pyre,
    But painful, plain, contracted observations:
    The gesture of a hand, dip of a bough

Or seven stubborn words drawn close together
As a hewn charm against the shifting weather.
    Our singing was intolerably sober
    Mistrusting every trill of artifice.

Whatever danced on needle-points, we knew
That we had forged the world we stumbled through
    And, if a stripped wind howled through sighing alleys,
    Built our own refuge in a flush of pride

Knowing that all our gifts were for construction –
Timber to timber groined in every section –
    And knowing, too, purged of the sense of evil,
    These were the walls our folly would destroy.

We dreamed, woke, doubted, wept for fading stars
And then projected brave new avatars,
    Triumphs of reason. Yet a whole dimension
    Had vanished from the chambers of the mind,

And paramount among the victims fled,
Shrunken and pale, the grim king of the dead;
    Withdrawn to caverns safely beyond our sounding
    He waits as a Pretender for his call,

Which those who crave him can no longer give.
Men are the arbiters of how they live,
  And, stooped by millstones of authority,
  They welcome tyrants in with open arms.

Now in the shadows of unfriendly trees
We number leaves, discern faint similes
  And learn to praise whatever is imperfect
  As the true breeding-ground for honesty,

Finding our heroism in rejection
Of bland Utopias and of thieves' affection:
  Our greatest joy to mark an outline truly
  And know the piece of earth on which we stand.

ELIZABETH BISHOP (*USA*)

The Man-Moth

....

Here, above,
cracks in the buildings are filled with battered moonlight.
The whole shadow of Man is only as big as his hat.
It lies at his feet like a circle for a doll to stand on,
and he makes an inverted pin, the point magnetised to the moon.
He does not see the moon; he observes only her vast properties,
feeling the queer light on his hands, neither warm nor cold,
of a temperature impossible to record in thermometers.

But when the Man-Moth
pays his rare, although occasional, visits to the surface,
the moon looks rather different to him. He emerges
from an opening under the edge of one of the sidewalks
and nervously begins to scale the faces of the buildings.
He thinks the moon is a small hole at the top of the sky,
proving the sky quite useless for protection.
He trembles, but must investigate as high as he can climb.

Up the façades,
his shadow dragging like a photographer's cloth behind him,
he climbs fearfully, thinking that this time he will manage
to push his small head through that round clean opening
and be forced through, as from a tube, in black scrolls on the light.
(Man, standing below him, has no such illusions.)
But what the Man-Moth fears most he must do, although
he fails, of course, and falls back scared but quite unhurt.

Then he returns
to the pale subways of cement he calls his home. He flits,
he flutters, and cannot get aboard the silent trains
fast enough to suit him. The doors close swiftly.
The Man-Moth always seats himself facing the wrong way
and the train starts at once at its full, terrible speed,
without a shift in gears or a gradation of any sort.
He cannot tell the rate at which he travels backwards.

Each night he must
be carried through artificial tunnels and dream recurrent dreams.
Just as the ties recur beneath his train, these underlie
his rushing brain. He does not dare look out the window,
for the third rail, the unbroken draught of poison,
runs there beside him. He regards it as a disease
he has inherited the susceptibility to. He has to keep
his hands in his pockets, as others must wear mufflers.

If you catch him,
hold up a flashlight to his eye. It's all dark pupil,
an entire night itself, whose haired horizon tightens
as he stares back, and closes up the eye. Then from the lids
one tear, his only possession, like a bee's sting, slips.
Slyly he palms it, and if you're not paying attention
he'll swallow it. However, if you watch, he'll hand it over,
cool as from underground springs and pure enough to drink.

R.A. SIMPSON (*Australia*)

Making a Myth

....

Making a myth is easy
if you are the first man
made to stand before a daybreak landscape
and near a laden tree growing greener:

and here you find the back-drop
stacked high with granite portraits
glaring at the foreground sand
etched with little ideograms
drawn finely like a spider's web:

and you decipher these as legends
and give the greening tree the name of Apple
while looking at the nearby hillocks
catching fire with careful flowers:

and so you make those flowers people
as you pause then slowly kneel
waiting for a distant answer
to this question:

"Father of the earth and sky;
long ago – was there a choice?"

But you only hear your voice:

an echo dying from the air;

and it's followed by a silence
you can't bear:

it's so immense.

Anna Akhmatova (*USSR*)

Prologue

···

(*From* 'Requiem')

In those years only the dead smiled,
Glad to be at rest:
And Leningrad city swayed like
A needless appendix to its prisons.
It was then that the railway yards
Were asylums of the mad;
Short were the locomotives'
Farewell songs.
Stars of death stood
Above us, and innocent Russia
Writhed under bloodstained boots, and
Under the tyres of Black Marias

Translated by D.M. Thomas

GRANDFATHER KOORI (*Australia*)

Massacre Sandhill

The rain the rain the rain
the rain upon the hill
the three horsemen came
the three horses
the rain came down in clouds
and cried
the rain the rain cried
until it washed the blood
back into the land again
the rain the rain cried
until there was only the drought.

CHRIS WALLACE-CRABBE (*Australia*)

Beijing
....

It is your blood again.

For a while we sat back
against the fond cushions of our belief
that civilisation might be possible,
could last,
was on the rise;
but the tanks,
the appalling tanks,
resume their sway
in squares and broken streets:
they roll over cries and falling selves.

The horrible old men roll over,
knowing they have to die
and have just a little while
to crush their juniors in a pond of blood,
to prevent the future from ever taking place.

DOAN VAN MINH (*Vietnam*)

When the policy changes
....

Whenever the policy changes
You would see PEOPLE covered by sweat
A 15-year-old girl offering herself in a deserted alley
Prisons mushroom all over the place
Aged mothers bent carrying hawking goods
Children talking back to father
Wife swearing back to husband
Dishonesties, and lies filling the Party newspaper
Whenever the policy changes
Nobody cares to teach POETRY, MUSIC, ART
But busy to teach people how to kill
To teach people how to make fox holes and trenches
A country full of hatred, impoverished by war
Surrounded by cheating and dishonesty
Whenever the policy changes
Land, rice paddy pushed into co-ops
Harvest time so quiet without folksongs
Peasants with faces as green as the rice plant
Burdened down with a hundred kinds of taxes
Personal tax, market tax etc, etc . . .
Damn city cluttered up with litter
Houses so noisy with laughter, crying and arguments
And smiles lingering with sorrow
Whenever the policy changes
You could see quite a lot of people spying on you
Quite a lot of guns pushing down the pens
Let's write about the future
Don't bother about the time being
No matter what kind of life we are living now

BASIL FERNANDO (*Sri Lanka*)

The anonymous people

We
Are the anonymous people
No photos
No paintings
To record our past
Our forefathers
Collected no stamps

No public wall
Bears our name
No awards of us
In public games
We
Are the anonymous people
our forefathers were the same

Age's suffering
Connects us to past
No memories of us
But our world is vast
We
Are the anonymous people
Silence is our mask

MARIN SORESCU (*Romania*)

Competition
....

One, two, three . . .
The hibernation competition has begun.
Everyone lock yourselves in your lair
And let's see who can hibernate the longest.

You know the competition rules:
No moving,
No dreaming,
No thinking.
Anyone caught thinking
Is out of the game and no longer our concern.

Like a pipe, you can only use
Your paw for sucking
To stimulate you in the deep understanding
Of this event.

I'm lucky to find myself near a bear,
Because when I've had enough of my paw,
I'll give it to him,
And use his,
Which as it happens is within the accepted norm
Of paws.
And although the Pharoah Cheops
Has the advantage of a few milleniums,
I also hope to overtake him
By an outstanding sprint,
Our famous sprint
In the field of hibernation.

Every year
Life salutes us
With 365 shots
Of sun.

It's a great event
Our arrival into the
Inanimate world,
And matter
Gives us our due
Honours.

The trees put on little flags
Of seasons,
In the air, rise oxygen bubbles
And coloured stars.

From the sea cheers are heard,
Waves carry banners.
Everything
Clamours to see us,
What more can I say?
It's a beautiful feast and unrivalled.

And we, moved,
For as long as the light lasts,
Stay standing
As for the national anthem.

Translated by Andrea Deletant and Brenda Walker

HORST BIENEK (*Germany*)

The Myth of Time

The myth of time disintegrates
The birds mourn softly in the wind
You chose the cell in which you sleep
That truth might live you passed the gates
And wedded to the dream you weep
The birds mourn softly in the wind
The myth of time disintegrates

Translated by Ruth and Matthew Mead

AHMAD FARAZ (*Pakistan*)

Don't Think

And she
pouring red wine into my glass,
said Don't think so much!
You're in a place now – in this country,
in this city – where you can enjoy yourself,
where everyone is dancing, singing, swinging.
Stop thinking, relax!
What sort of people are you?
Even when you go abroad
you bring your sickly night and day,
your broken heart, your memories of friends,
like your soiled torn shirts
whose stains cannot be cleaned
by the machines of laundries –
these scars of poverty,
this self-destructive darkness of the soul
this self-neglect, you carry them
as if they were dear to you!
But here where you are now,
life is no dream,
nor a whirlpool of thought;
life here is like wine – daring, seductive,
not a poison.
Leave your begging-bowl at the doorstep,
begging is not the done thing here,
relax,
don't think so much!

Translated by Mahmood Jamal

ROBERT ADAMSON (*Australia*)

Canticle For The Bicentennial Dead

They are talking, in their cedar-benched rooms
on French-polished chairs, and they talk

in reasonable tones, in the great stone buildings
they are talking firmly, in the half-light

and they mention at times the drinking of alcohol,
the sweet blood-coloured wine the young drink,

the beer they share in the riverless river-beds
and the backstreets, and in the main street –

in government coloured parks, drinking
the sweet blood in recreation patches, campsites.

They talk, the clean-handed ones, as they gather
strange facts; and as they talk

collecting words, they sweat under nylon wigs.
Men in blue uniforms are finding the bodies,

the Uniforms are finding the dead: young hunters
who have lost their hunting, singers who

would sing of fish, are now found hung –
crumpled in night-rags in the public's corners;

discovered there broken, illuminated by stripes
of regulated sunlight beneath the whispering

rolling cell-window bars. Their bodies
found in postures of human-shaped effigies,

hunched in the dank sour urinated atmosphere
near the bed-board, beside cracked lavatory bowls

slumped on the thousand-grooved, fingernailed walls
of your local Police Station's cell –

Bodies of the street's larrikin Koories
suspended above concrete in the phenyl-thick air.

Meanwhile outside the count continues, on radio
the TV news; like Vietnam again, the faces

of mothers torn across the screens –
And the poets write no elegies, our artists

cannot describe the shape of their grief, though
the clean-handed ones paginate dossiers

and court reporter's hands move over the papers.

ANNA AKHMATOVA (*USSR*)

Why is our century worse than any other?

Why is our century worse than any other?
Is it that in the stupor of fear and grief
It has plunged its fingers in the blackest ulcer,
Yet cannot bring relief?

Westward the sun is dropping,
And the roofs of towns are shining in its light.
Already death is chalking doors with crosses
And calling the ravens and the ravens are in flight.

[1919]

Translated by D.M. Thomas

JUDITH WRIGHT (*Australia*)

Weapon

The will to power destoys the power to will.
The weapon made, we cannot help but use it;
it drags us with its own momentum still.

The power to kill compounds the need to kill.
Grown out of hand, the heart cannot refuse it;
the will to power undoes the power to will.

Though as we strike we cry "I did not choose it",
it drags us with its own momentum still.
In the one stroke we win the world and lose it.
The will to power destroys the power to will.

ROBERT GRAY (*Australia*)

Karl Marx

....

Karl Marx was playing a parlour game
with his daughters. To their question
What is the quality one should most abhor?
he wrote: Servility.

This was found – a scrap of paper
amongst the family albums and letters;
it is the most essential of all
the Complete Works.

CLARIBEL ALEGRÍA (*El Salvador*)

Little Cambray Tamales

··

(*makes 5,000,000 little tamales*)

for Eduardo and Helena who asked me
for a Salvadoran recipe

Two pounds of mestizo cornmeal
half a pound of loin of *gachupin*
cooked and finely chopped
a box of pious raisins
two tablespoons of Malinche milk
one cup of enraged water
a fry of conquistador helmets
three Jesuit onions
a small bag of multinational gold
two dragon's teeth
one presidential carrot
two tablespoons of pimps
lard of Panchimalco Indians
two ministerial tomatoes
a half cup of television sugar
two drops of volcanic lava
seven leaves of *pito*
(don't be dirty-minded, it's a soporific)
put everything to boil
over a slow fire
for five hundred years
and you'll see how tasty it is.

Translated by D.J. Flakoll

HORST BIENEK (*Germany*)

Vorkuta
....

In Vorkuta no disciple of the Lord
walks the green-foaming tundra.
Here there is no feeding of the five thousand.
Here a dream dies every day
in the still uncertain dawn.

In Vorkuta, no machine-guns rust.
Whoever tires listens to the cantata
of the snowstorm in the barbed wire
and embroiders with his own blood
an endless pattern in his black katorga-shirt.

Nor in Vorkuta
is the prayer of the dead a prayer
and the lips of the living
are rusting lips, iron bars,
behind which the tongue festers and rots.

In Vorkuta no widow
covers her hair with a veil.
Her breasts still tremble
when she thinks of the loneliness
beneath the arching body of a man.

In Vorkuta no one digs a grave
for crumbling hopes
And there is no one to weep
when the abandoned corpses
drift to the rivers with the melting snow.

[VORKUTA, 1953]

Translated by Ruth and Matthew Mead

JÁNOS PILINSZKY (*Hungary*)

Apocrypha

···

1

Everything will be forsaken then
The silence of the heavens will be set apart
and forever apart
the broken-down fields of the finished world,
and apart
the silence of dog-kennels.
In the air a fleeing host of birds.
And we shall see the rising sun
dumb as a demented eye-pupil
and calm as a watching beast.

But keeping vigil in banishment
because that night
I cannot sleep I toss
as the tree with its thousand leaves
and at dead of night I speak as the tree:

Do you know the drifting of the years
the years over the crumpled fields?
Do you understand the wrinkle
of transience? Do you comprehend
my care-gnarled hands? Do you know
the name of orphanage? Do you know
what pain treads the unlifting darkness
with cleft hooves, with webbed feet?
The night, the cold, the pit. Do you know
the convict's head twisted askew?
Do you know the caked troughs, the tortures
of the abyss?

The sun rose. Sticks of trees blackening
in the infra-red of the wrathful sky.

So I depart. Facing devastation
a man is walking, without a word.
He has nothing. He has his shadow.
And his stick. And his prison garb.

2

And this is why I learned to walk! For these
belated bitter steps.

Evening will come, and night will petrify
above me with its mud. Beneath closed eyelids
I do not cease to guard this procession
these fevered shrubs, their tiny twigs.
Leaf by leaf, the glowing little wood.
Once Paradise stood here.
In half-sleep, the renewal of pain:
to hear its gigantic trees.

Home – I wanted finally to get home –
to arrive as he in the Bible arrived.
My ghastly shadow in the courtyard.
Crushed silence, aged parents in the house.
And already they are coming, they are calling me,
my poor ones, and already crying,
and embracing me, stumbling –
the ancient order opens to readmit me.
I lean out on the windy stars.

If only for this once I could speak with you
whom I loved so much. Year after year
yet I never tired of saying over
what a small child sobs
into the gap between the palings,
the almost choking hope
that I come back and find you.
Your nearness throbs in my throat.
I am agitated as a wild beast.

(*contd*)

I do not speak your words,
the human speech. There are birds alive
who flee now heart-broken
under the sky, under the fiery sky.
Forlorn poles stuck in a glowing field,
and immovably burning cages.
I do not understand the human speech,
and I do not speak your language.
My voice is more homeless than the word!
I have no words.

            Its horrible burden
tumbles down through the air –
a tower's body emits sounds.

You are nowhere. How empty the world is.
A garden chair, and a deckchair left outside.
Among sharp stones my clangorous shadow.
I am tired. I jut out from the earth.

3

God sees that I stand in the sun.
He sees my shadow on stone and on fence.
He sees my shadow standing
without a breath in the airless press.

By then I am already like the stone;
a dead fold, a drawing of a thousand grooves,
a good handful of rubble
is by then the creature's face.

And instead of tears, the wrinkles on the faces
trickling, the empty ditch trickles down.

Translated by János Csokits and Ted Hughes

KEVIN HART (*Australia*)

The Twenty-first Century

When we arrive there
with our guns, our machinery, our heavy books,
there will be so much to say,

and we will sit down
over cigars and cognac and tell our stories
of minor battles, mirages, times when it seemed
no one would survive.

And we will talk only about ourselves,
forgetting our fathers
and all they did, their belief that the future
was only as good
as their plans for it,
and that we grew to be the same.

Then we can finish our stories in peace,
when the wars
are no longer ours to fight,

when we no longer have the clenched fists
of our youth, and our children have inherited
the terrible certainty
that we have ruined all we have been given,

and our hands will be empty,
we will have nothing to give, only our stories
of how everything we should have held before us
like a candle
was lost, forgotten, as we made our way
across the fields of sadness, walking towards the horizon.

NINA CASSIAN (*Romania*)

Horizon

And yet there must exist
a zone of salvation.
Sad are the countries
who don't have outlets to water,
dull are the people who have no outlet from themselves
toward another outlet, even greater.

Translated by Andrea Deletant and Brenda Walker

It takes much time to kill a tree

> The hand that signed the paper felled a city;
> Five sovereign fingers taxed the breath,
> Doubled the globe of dead and halved a country;
> These five kings did a king to death.

DYLAN THOMAS

GIEVE PATEL (*India*)

On Killing a Tree

It takes much time to kill a tree,
Not a simple jab of the knife
Will do it. It has grown
Slowly consuming the earth,
Rising out of it, feeding
Upon its crust, absorbing
Years of sunlight, air, water,
And out of its leprous hide
Sprouting leaves.

So hack and chop
But this alone won't do it.
Not so much pain will do it.
The bleeding bark will heal
And from close to the ground
Will rise curled green twigs,
Miniature boughs
Which if unchecked will expand again
To former size.

No,
The root is to be pulled out –
Out of the anchoring earth;
It is to be roped, tied,
And pulled out – snapped out
Or pulled out entirely,
Out from the earth-cave,
And the strength of the tree exposed,
The source, white and wet,
The most sensitive, hidden
For years inside the earth.

Then the matter
Of scorching and choking
In sun and air,
Browning, hardening,
Twisting, withering,

And then it is done.

TSUBOI SHIGEJI (*Japan*)

Silent, but . . .
....

I MAY be silent, but
I'm thinking.
I may not talk, but
Don't mistake me for a wall.

Translated by Geoffrey Bownan and Anthony Thwaite

LIANG XIAOBIN (*China*)

The Snow-White Wall

Mother,
I saw a snow-white wall.

This morning I went up the street to buy crayons
And I saw a workman
Striving with all his might
To whitewash a long enclosure wall.

He looked and smiled over his shoulder at me,
And he asked me to tell all the children:
    Don't scribble a mess on the wall anymore.

Mother,
I saw a snow-white wall.

That wall used to be filthy,
Scrawled with many violent, brutal words.
Mother, you once wept
Over those very curses.

Daddy is gone,
Gone forever.

The wall that's so white,
Whiter than the milk I drink,
Has been flashing through my dreams.
It stands on the horizon
Shimmering with enchanting light in the daytime.
I love pure white.

I'll never draw a mess on the wall,
Never will.
Blue sky, gentle as my Mother –
Did you hear me?

Mother,
I saw a snow-white wall.

[MAY-AUGUST 1980]

Translated by Fang Dai, Dennis Ding and Edward Morin

KISHWAR NAHEED (*Pakistan*)

Listen To Me
....

If you want to speak
your punishment is death.
If you want to breathe
your place is in the prison.
If you want to walk
then cut off your legs
and carry them in your arms.
If you want to laugh
hang upside down in a well.
If you want to think
then shut all the doors
and throw away the key.
If you want to cry
then sink into the river.
If you want to live
then become a cobweb on the cave
of your dreams.
And if you want to forget everything
then pause and think:
of the word you first learnt.

Translated by Mahmood Jamal

SAUL YURKIEVICH (*Argentina*)

Sentence

doesn't read what he should
thinks what he shouldn't
doesn't say what he should
writes what he shouldn't

shouldn't read
shouldn't think
shouldn't speak
shouldn't write

should read what he should
should think what he should
should say what he should
should write what he should

what he shouldn't do is read
what he shouldn't do is think
what he shouldn't do is speak
what he shouldn't do is write

doesn't live as he should
lives but shouldn't
shouldn't live

Translated by Cola Franzen

IVAN KRAUS (*Czechoslovakia*)

The Censor

The Censor is seated on a stool (or possibly two stools).
The Dancer enters.
At a sign from the Censor she begins to dance.
Censor: More slowly, please.
The Dancer continues to dance.
The Censor stops her.
Censor: Hold it! Show me that last movement again.
The Dancer does so.
The Censor shakes his head.
Censor: No, no, no. Leave that out.
The Dancer resumes her dance.
Censor: No. Not that. Omit it.
The Dancer dances.
Censor: That's not allowed.
The Dancer again resumes dancing.
Censor: Omit!
(after a while)
    Omit!
(after a while)
    Leave out!
(after a while)
    And that!
The Dancer no longer dances, she is merely walking about
    the stage.
Censor: What's this? Call that a dance? Why aren't you dancing?
The Dancer shrugs her shoulders helplessly.
Censor: Don't do that!
The Curtain starts to come down.
Censor: Just a moment!
The Curtain stops.
Censor: I won't stand for any innuendo. Gently, now . . .
    that's better . . . gently . . . very, very slowly . . .

The End

Translated by George Theiner

DAVID RAY (*USA*)

Propaganda

How quickly the victors
rewrite history.
The big lie works.
Tell it again and again
loud and clear
as the truth seldom is.
There was no massacre
in Tiananmen Square
says the Chinese state radio
and within a week
National Public Radio
in Washington, DC,
says they have to agree,
see no hard evidence.
It is true – no massacre
in Tiananmen Square!
The new truth from China
is affirmed – "It never
happened that soldiers
fired directly
at the people."
But I still can't get
out of my eyes that sight
broadcast on TV to millions –
islands of blood –
truly a thousand red islands
in Tiananmen Square.
We saw it. Yet now
we are told
it did not happen
and the kids
are rounded up
as they were in Budapest.
The Chinese people are told
it did not happen.
We are told.

We begin to forget.
We agree to forget.
It does not take long
to fulfil our contract
to forget. Bloodstains
on stone – who remembers them
past a fortnight?
Not you, not me,
not the Chinese state radio,
not the USA state radio.
How quickly indeed
the victors rewrite!
Propaganda works – that is all
the truth ye know
and all ye need to know.

CECIL RAJENDRA (*Malaysia*)

The Animal and Insect Act

Finally, in order to ensure
absolute national security
they passed the Animal and Insect
Emergency Control and Discipline Act.

Under this new Act, buffaloes
cows and goats were prohibited
from grazing in herds of more
than three. Neither could birds
flock, nor bees swarm . . .
This constituted unlawful assembly.

As they had not obtained prior
planning permission, mud-wasps
and swallows were issued with
summary Notices to Quit. Their
homes were declared subversive
extensions to private property.

Monkeys and mynahs were warned
to stop relaying their noisy
morning orisons until an official
Broadcasting Licence was issued
by the appropriate Ministry.
Unmonitored publications and broad-
casts posed the gravest threats
in times of a National Emergency.

Similarly, woodpeckers had
to stop tapping their morse-
code messages from coconut
tree-top to chempaka tree.

All messages were subject
to a thorough pre-scrutiny
by the relevant authorities.

Java sparrows were arrested in
droves for rumour-mongering.
Cats (suspected of conspiracy)
had to be indoors by 9 o'clock
Cicadas and crickets received
notification to turn their amp-
lifiers down. Ducks could not
quack nor turkeys gobble during
restricted hours. Need I say,
all dogs – alsatians, dachshunds,
terriers, pointers and even
little chihuahuas – were muzzled.

In the interests of security
penguins and zebras were
ordered to discard their
non-regulation uniforms.
The deer had to surrender
their dangerous antlers.
Tigers and all carnivores
with retracted claws were
sent directly to prison
for concealing lethal weapons.

And by virtue of Article
Four, paragraph 2(b)
sub-section sixteen,
under no circumstances
were elephants allowed
to break wind between
the hours of six and six.
Their farts could easily
be interpreted as gunshot.
Might spark off a riot . . .

(contd)

A month after the Act
was properly gazetted
the birds and insects
started migrating south
the animals went north
and an eerie silence
handcuffed our forests.

There was now Total Security.

JAMES MCAULEY (*Australia*)

Jindyworobaksheesh

By the waters of Babylon
I heard a Public Works official say:
"A culture that is truly Babylonian
Has been ordered for delivery today."

By the waters of Babylon
A quiet noise of subsidies in motion.
"To a bald or mangy surface we apply
Our sovereign art-provoking lotion."

By the waters of Babylon I heard
That art was for the people; but they meant
That art should sweeten to the people's mouth
The droppings from the perch of government.

MIRCEA DINESCU (*Romania*)

Cold Comfort

God preserve me from those who want what's best for me
from the nice guys
always cheerfully ready to inform on me
from the priest with a tape recorder under his vestment
from the blanket you can't get under without saying good evening
from the dictators caught in the chords of the harp
from those angry with their own people
now when winter's coming
we have neither tall walls
nor geese on the Capitoline
only great provisions of tolerance and fear

Translated by Brenda Walker and Andrea Deletant

D.H. LAWRENCE (*UK*)

Censors

....

Censors are dead men
set up to judge between life and death.
For no live, sunny man would be a censor,
he'd just laugh.

But censors, being dead men,
have a stern eye on life.
– That thing's alive! It's dangerous. Make away
     with it! –
And when the execution is performed
you hear the stertorous, self-righteous heavy
     breathing of the dead men,
the censors, breathing with relief.

YANNIS RITSOS (*Greece*)

Search

Come in, Gentlemen – he said. No inconvenience. Look through
    everything;
I have nothing to hide. Here's the bedroom, here the study,
here the dining-room. Here? – the attic for old things; –
everything wears out, Gentlemen; it's full; everything wears out,
    wears out,
so quickly too, Gentlemen; this? – a thimble; – mother's;
this? mother's oil-lamp, mother's umbrella – she loved me
    enormously; –
but this forged identity card? this jewellery, somebody else's? the
    dirty towel?
this theatre ticket? the shirt with holes? blood stains?
and this photograph? his, yes, wearing a woman's hat covered
    with flowers,
inscribed to a stranger – his handwriting –
who planted these in here? who planted these in here? who
    planted these in here?

Translated by Nikos Stangos

TSUBOI SHIGEJI (*Japan*)

English – ugh!

One morning, reading the paper, I was flabbergasted.
A well-known singer
On his way home on pay-day,
Was set on by hot-headed Fascists
In a bar
Because, a bit out of sorts,
He sang his favorite song in English.

What a suspicious world it is!
But how about
Those Fascists drinking
Un-Japanese beer? Interesting!

I read the report and thought:
If these bastards
Hate English all that much,
As revenge, and to test the skill of their thugs,
How would it be if, from end to end of Japan,
They set on, one by one,
All who speak English?

The immediate quarry would be the teacher of English.
Japan may well be narrow, but
She is a land where education booms;
There might be one, two, thousand teachers of English.
So, however mailed the Fascists' fists,
They'd have no end of trouble.

I remembered that
The Franco-Anglo-Japanese Girls' School in Kanda
Had been renamed – the sweeter-scented Academy of the White Lily.
Before our 'State of Emergency', this girls' school
Went by its first name, with
France at the head,
England for its body
And Japan, the vital part,
Down at the feet. Scandalous! Insult!

So, when all was said and done, it had to be
The Girls' Academy of the White Lily.
Well! By such penman's logic
What on earth happens to dictionary names?
'Japanese-English dictionary' may pass,
But how about 'English-Japanese dictionary'?
Bloody English
French
German
Russian
Any foreign language!
Get out of Japan right now!
Then
Our Fascists can be at ease
And take their time over their beer in bars,
Getting tight,
Uninterrupted by songs in English,
Bellowing out our own songs.

Who is he?
– The bastard who keeps yarping that 'bar' is English?
Isn't there a worthy Japanese word for it? –
Sake-spot.
And the beer they're drinking?
That is barley-brew.
Or, rather, wheat-wine to our Fascist friends.   ·

Translated by Geoffrey Bownas and Anthony Thwaite

Mykola Rudenko (*USSR*)

It's so easy: just recant

It's so easy: just recant
And restore your right to live.
A dozen words or maybe phrases
And yesterday will suddenly be brought back:
The trees and flowers in shimmering dew,
And children's voices outside the window;
The fish in the lake and birds in the sky,
And the taste of a kiss on your lips
As proof of love and goodness that exists . . .
Only you no longer will be the same.
Hunched and grown pale from illness,
Just an empty shell without a soul.
Try on the old suits once more,
And get the most out of your study-haven.
Tramp up and down the garden path –
But you won't retrieve the soul you've lost.
Just a dozen words forced out while half-awake
And you are no more,
Just emptiness –
A dungeon concealed in a man.

Translated by Irena Eva Mostovych

DENNIS BRUTUS (*South Africa*)

The Sounds Begin Again

The sounds begin again;
the siren in the night
the thunder at the door
the shriek of nerves in pain.

      Then the keening crescendo
      of faces split by pain
      the wordless, endless wail
      only the unfree know.

            Importunate as rain
            the wraiths exhale their woe
            over the sirens, knuckles, boots;
            my sounds begin again.

METIJA BEĆKOVIĆ (*Yugoslavia*)

If I knew I'd bear myself proudly

If I knew I'd bear myself proudly
Before judges and serving my sentence,
What a trail I'd blaze and endure everything,
Warding it all off with my bare limbs.

If I knew I'd kick the table alone
Under my feet and fix the noose myself,
My soul would earn itself eternity
And my hangman go on weeping after me.

But I'm afraid, I'd start to beg,
To sob, to kneel, to betray everything,
Just to save my bare ass,
I'd spit on all and agree to everything.

Translated by Charles Simic

GYÖRGY PETRI (*Hungary*)

To be said over and over again

I glance down at my shoe and – there's the lace!
This can't be gaol then, can it, in that case.

Translated by George Gömöri and Clive Wilmer

IV

···

Last night . . . I disappeared

I saw the world, and yet I was not seen:
My thread is cut, and yet it is not spun;
And now I live, and now my life is done.

CHIDIOCK TICHBORNE

ANA IRIS VARAS (*Chile*)

Untitled

Love
last night I forgot everything
I left for nowhere
I disappeared,
and became
a little speck on the stove . . .
only the music remained,
its rhythm and you
on my mind.
I didn't exist
I'd disappeared
slipping into the sound wave
quivering in the air
trying to reach you.

Translated by John Kraniauskas

ROBERTO SABALLOS (*El Salvador*)

A Story

··

To my sister, María Teresa Saballos, disappeared by the
National Guard on September 15, 1979.

This is the story of María Teresa
of her weary days
and her long nights
of her lone mother
and her young son
this is the story of her boredom
of her slow steps
and her black hair
her open smile
and her old-woman's hands.

This is her story
with more grief than happiness
with fewer years than sadnesses.
This is the story of her goodbye
of her farewell without farewells.

This is the story of her mother
of her useless steps
of her quiet waiting from jail to jail
from court to court
with smiling judges
who are empty-handed.

This is the story of her eyes
that peer at her hair
her clear gaze
and her strong hands
that were lost long ago
in the cold dawn
this is the story of María Teresa
this is the story of my people.

Translated by Claribel Alegría and Darwin J. Flakoll

AHMAD FARAZ (*Pakistan*)

Beirut

Whose headless body is this
whose scarlet shroud
whose torn and wounded cloak
whose broken voice?

Whose blood is this
that turns the earth a ruby colour,
whose cruel embrace
taking the coffin's shape?

Who are these youths
standing in the line of fire,
what city are they from?

Who are these helpless ones
lying scattered
like a harvest reaped
by enemy swords?

Whose faces have we here,
drops of blood like pearls
glistening on their lips and eyes?

Who is this mother
searching in the debris
for her child,
who is this father
his voice lost
in the terrible chaos?

Who are these innocent ones
extinguished
like lamps
by the dark storm?

Which tribe are they from,
these brave people
ready to die?
No one wants to know them
for knowing them
is like a test;
we see no child, no mother,
no father in their midst.

In the palaces
the lucky sheikhs are silent;
kings are silent,
protectors of the faith,
rulers of the world,
all silent.
All these hypocrites
who take God's name
are silent!

Translated by Mahmood Jamal

MARCOS ANA (*Spain*)

A Short Letter to the World

(*extract from* From Burgos Jail)

Gripped in a crossbow's teeth
I am held and cannot fly.

My soul is torn
by its struggle to break free
but I cannot pull out these bolts
that have been shot home through my breast. . . .

You do not know what a man is
torn and bleeding in a snare.
If you knew it you would come
on the waves and on the wind
out of every borderland
with your hearts melting and sick
holding up your fists aloft
come to rescue what is yours.

If one day you come too late
and you find my body cold,
if you find my comrades dead
white as snow among their chains,
pick our banners up again
and our anguish and our dreams
and the names upon the walls
which we carved with loving care. . . .

If one day you come too late
and you find my body cold
look among the lonely places
in the wall to find my will:
to the world I do bequeath
all I have and all I feel
all I was among my kind
all I am and all I stand for:

one banner that brings no sorrow
one love, a little verse . . .
and on the lacerating stones
of this grey yard which none will enter
my cry to stand like an appalling
scarlet statue in the centre.

Translated by Chloe Vulliamy and Stephen Sedley

MIROSLAV HOLUB (*Czechoslovakia*)

Waiting

The one who waits is always the mother,
all her fingers jammed
    in the automatic doors of the world,
all her thoughts like
    egg-laden moths pinned out alive,
and in her bag the mirror shows
    time long gone by when
    glad cries lingered in the apple trees,
and at home the spool and the thread are whispering together:
    What will become of us?

The one who waits is always the mother,
and a thousand things whose fate is
    ineluctable fall.

The one who waits is always the mother,
    smaller and smaller,
    fading and fading
    second by second,
until in the end
    no one sees her.

Translated by I. Milner and G. Theinier

RENATA PALLOTTINI (*Brazil*)

The Shriek

If at least this pain helped
if it knocked walls
if it opened doors
if it spoke
if it sang and uncombed my hair

if at least this pain saw itself
if it sprung from the throat like a shriek
if it fell from the window if it would burst
if it would die

if the pain were a piece of hard bread
one could swallow with strength
and spit out after
stain the street the cars the space the other
that dark other which passes indifferently
and does not suffer who has a right not to suffer

if pain were only finger flesh
which can be rubbed on stone wall
so it hurts hurts visibly
painfully
with tears

if at least this pain would bleed

Translated by Carlos and Monique Altschul

W.S. MERWIN (*USA*)

Some Last Questions

What is the head
      a.   Ash
What are the eyes
      a.   The wells have fallen in and have
              Inhabitants
What are the feet
      a.   Thumbs left after the auction
No what are the feet
      a.   Under them the impossible road is moving
              Down which the broken necked mice push
              Balls of blood with their noses
What is the tongue
      a.   The black coat that fell off the wall
              With sleeves trying to say something
What are the hands
      a.   Paid
No what are the hands
      a.   Climbing back down the museum wall
              To their ancestors the extinct shrews that will
              Have left a message
What is the silence
      a.   As though it has a right to more
Who are the compatriots
      a.   They make the stars of bone

CZESLAW MILOSZ (*Poland*)

Dedication

You whom I could not save
Listen to me.
Try to understand this simple speech as I would be
    ashamed of another.
I swear, there is in me no wizardry of words.
I speak to you with silence like a cloud or a tree.

What strengthened me, for you was lethal.
You mixed up farewell to an epoch with the beginning
    of a new one,
Inspiration of hatred with lyrical beauty,
Blind force with accomplished shape.

Here is the valley of shallow Polish rivers. And an
    immense bridge
Going into white fog. Here is a broken city,
And the wind throws screams of gulls on your grave
When I am talking with you.

What is poetry which does not save
Nations or people?
A connivance with official lies,
A song of drunkards whose throats will be cut in a
    moment,
Readings for sophomore girls.
That I wanted good poetry without knowing it,
That I discovered, late, its salutary aim,
In this and only this I find salvation.

They used to pour on graves millet or poppy seeds
To feed the dead who would come disguised as birds.
I put this book here for you, who once lived
So that you should visit us no more.

GARY GEDDES (*Canada*)

General Cemetery

Between the wrought-iron crosses of the disappeared
are no bored lions, avenues of eucalyptus;
here none go down to corruption

in the splendid isolation of crypt or mausoleum,
where empty skulls imagine their importance
and bones are wont to speak of privilege.

Between the wrought-iron crosses of the disappeared
you'll find no tributes to the intellect,
no verse inscriptions, no trace of Greece or Egypt

in the architecture. Add up the ragged columns
of the dispossessed and let archival winds
record each article of faith.

Between the wrought-iron crosses of the disappeared
only a half-starved dog can pass,
or a humming-bird, his heart in his throat.

He hovers overlong above the opened grave,
bearing witness to travesties
that do not stop with death in Santiago.

A woman's square-heeled shoe protrudes
from heaps of brick and bone, a patch of colour
showing through the skein of dust.

Between the wrought-iron crosses of the disappeared
her plastic heels are platforms of dissent;
her wit and candour, crimes against the state.

Place your flower gently now among the nameless dead
and let its beauty fade, its cut throat bleed,
into the silent, unassuming earth.

MARJORIE AGOSIN (*Chile*)

Disappeared Woman 1

I am the disappeared woman,
in a country grown dark,
silenced by the
wrathful cubbyholes
of those with no memory.
You still don't see me?
You still don't hear me
in those peregrinations
through the dense smoke
of terror?
Look at me,
nights, days, soundless tomorrows
sing me
so that no one may
threaten me
call me
to give me back
name,
sounds,
a covering of skin
by naming me.

Don't conspire with
oblivion,
tear down the silence.
I want to be
the appeared woman
from among the labyrinths
come back, return
name myself.
Call my name.

Translated by Cola Franzen

ARIEL DORFMAN (*Chile*)

Last Will and Testament

When they tell you
I'm not a prisoner
don't believe them.
They'll have to admit it
some day.
When they tell you
they released me
don't believe them.
They'll have to admit
it's a lie
some day.
When they tell you
I betrayed the party
don't believe them.
They'll have to admit
I was loyal
some day.
When they tell you
I'm in France
don't believe them.
Don't believe them when they show you
my false I.D.
don't believe them.
Don't believe them when they show you
the photo of my body,
don't believe them.
Don't believe them when they tell you
the moon is the moon,
if they tell you the moon is the moon,
that this is my voice on tape,
that this is my signature on a confession,
if they say a tree is a tree
don't believe them,
don't believe
anything they tell you

anything they swear to
anything they show you,
don't believe them.

And finally
when
that day
comes
when they ask you
to identify the body
and you see me
and a voice says
we killed him
the poor bastard died
he's dead,
when they tell you
that I am
completely absolutely definitely
dead
don't believe them,
don't believe them,
don't believe them.

Translated by Edie Grossman

DESANKA MAKSIMOVIĆ (*Yugoslavia*)

Now it is certain

Through the same gate I shall enter too.
The shadow will rush toward me
as one always rushes to a newcomer
arriving from the region
from which we were banished.

Their faces will be both different
and the same,
as every night the face of the moon
is different and the same again.

But I shall recognise your faces
were they woven of darkness
or shining with an inner glow;
they'll give themselves away by a small sign,
perhaps by a smile they had on the earth,
perhaps by the familiar sorrow in the eyes,
perhaps by the arch of the eyebrow.

Translated by Vasa Mihailovich

V

Darkness begets itself

When the burnt flesh is finally at rest,
The fires in the asylum grates will come up
And wicks turn down to darkness in the madman's
eyes.

PETER PORTER

WOLE SOYINKA (*Nigeria*)

The Apotheosis of Master Sergeant Doe

Welcome, dear Master Sergeant to the fold
Your pace was firm, your passage mean and bold.

Lean your entry, in studied Savior's form
Combat fatigued, self-styled a cleansing storm.

Let other shoulders sprout gold epaulettes
You shunned those status-greedy etiquettes,

Stayed simple Master Sergeant. The nation knew
Who was the Master; the Sergeants rendered due.

The comrade band diminished. The bloody contest played
Its grand finale. Alone the Master planner stayed

The course. The lean had rounded out. The barrack slob,
Close-crop peak-cap head affects new heartthrob

Swinger images. The tie pins are no paste.
The spoils of office, easy acquired taste

Distend the appetite, contract the scruples.
A crow may answer eagle, perched on borrowed steeples.

Flown on flags, graced by diplomatic corps
We consecrate the nightmare, kiss a nation's sore.

To mask the real, the world is turned a stage,
A rampant play of symbols masks a people's rage.

The ass that mimes the Lord's anointed wears
A face that once was human, prone to fears

But crowns are crowns. When rulers meet, their embraces
Are of presence. Absent cries make empty phrases.

The pile is high on that red carpet trail
That muffs the steps to your Inaugural Grail,

Skulls like cobbles, bones like harmattan twigs
The squeals of humans dying the death of pigs.

You missed the hisses too; a fanfare covers all.
The whine of violins at the State House Ball

Bears down the whining discords of misrule.
You've proved a grade A pupil from survivors' school.

Your worthy predecessors raise a toast
From exiled havens, or from the eternal roast

Swinging Bokassa, Macias Nguema, Idi Amin Dada
You sucked their teats, you supped from their cannibal larder,

And belched in unison. The pinnacle attained,
Next goal is duration. Shall we see you ordained

In the *Guinness Book of Records*, the Master stayer?
Youth is your ally, and appetite of a Master slayer.

Till the people's fiesta: a blood-red streamer
In Monrovian skies, a lamppost and – the swinging
                                        Redeemer.

Osip Mandelstam (*USSR*)

The Stalin Epigram

Our lives no longer feel ground under them.
At ten paces you can't hear our words.

But whenever there's a snatch of talk
it turns to the Kremlin mountaineer,

the ten thick worms his fingers,
his words like measures of weight,

the huge laughing cockroaches on his top lip,
the glitter of his boot-rims.

Ringed with a scum of chicken-necked bosses
he toys with the tributes of half-men.

One whistles, another meouws, a third snivels.
He pokes out his finger and he alone goes boom.

He forges decrees in a line like horseshoes,
One for the groin, one the forehead, temple, eye.

He rolls the executions on his tongue like berries.
He wishes he could hug them like big friends from home.

[November 1933]

Translated by Clarence Brown and W.S. Merwin

GYÖRGY PETRI (*Hungary*)

Night song of the personal shadow

The rain is pissing down,
you scum.
And you, you are asleep
in your nice warm room –
that or stuffing the bird.
Me? Till six in the morning
I rot in the slackening rain.
I must wait for my relief, I've got to wait
till you crawl out of your hole,
get up from beside your old woman.
So the dope can be passed on
as to where you've flown.
You are flying, spreading your wings.
Don't you get into my hands –
I'll pluck you while you're in flight.
This sodding rain
is something I won't forget,
my raincoat swelling
double its normal weight
and the soles of my shoes.
While you
were arsing around
in the warm room.

The time will come
when I feed you to fish in the Danube.

Translated by George Gömöri and Clive Wilmer

MBUYISENI OSWALD MTSHALI (*South Africa*)

Nightfall in Soweto

Nightfall comes like
a dreaded disease
seeping through the pores
of a healthy body
and ravaging it beyond repair.

A murderer's hand,
lurking in the shadows,
clasping a dagger,
strikes down the helpless victim.

I am the victim.
I am slaughtered
every night in the streets.
I am cornered by the fear
gnawing at my timid heart;
in my helplessness I languish.

Man has ceased to be man,
Man has become beast,
Man has become prey.

I am the prey;
I am the quarry to be run down
by the marauding beast
let loose by cruel nightfall
from his cage of death.

Where is my refuge?
Where am I safe?
Not in my matchbox house
where I barricade myself against nightfall.

I tremble at his crunching footsteps,
I quake at his deafening knock at the door.
"Open up!" he barks like a rabid dog
thirsty for my blood.

Nightfall! Nightfall!
You are my mortal enemy.
But why were you ever created?
Why can't it be daytime?
Daytime for evermore?

ERNESTO CARDENAL (*Nicaragua*)

Somoza Unveils The Statue Of Somoza In Somoza Stadium

It's not that I think the people erected this statue
because I know better than you that I ordered it myself.
Nor do I pretend to pass into posterity with it
because I know the people will topple it over someday.
Not that I wanted to erect to myself in life
the monument you never would erect to me in death:
I erected this statue because I knew you would hate it.

Translated by Steven F. White

LUPENGA MPHANDE (*Malawi*)

Song of a Prison Guard

I see you, prisoner of Dzeleka,
From behind this hole in the door panel;
I lurk along the hum of cicadas and mosquitoes
In moonshades of maize stalks and banana leaves
And shadows of barbed-wire posts and farm ridges.
I hide behind this iron cleft, and peep
Into your cell like a Cyclops, unseen –
I am guard to this humid valley prison camp.

Your little room, prisoner of Dzeleka,
Will grow forever small, your life in the lurch to waste
And cluck at the wind; even at night I will keep you awake
With the dry double lock designed to lacerate your sleep.
Don't tell me the political layout of your crimes;
I only stoke up furnaces for those I receive to roast
In chilly cells, and whet the axe for the condemned
To throttle at the gallows like a chick with its head off –
I am the guard charged with executions.

Do you see that window up the cell wall,
Prisoner of Dzeleka? Of course it's too small and will forever
Grow smaller, but look out sometimes on fine days;
If you find it painful to see children at play, and
Watch the life you've so unwittingly deserted, then study:
Count threads in a cobweb, rate the beams in a ray from
The crack on the eastern wall at break of day
Study the ray that lingers on after nightfall,
Study the strands in a life that's lost its shadow, study . . .

And when you discover the beam-wave that relates to your pain
Hum in harmony with cicadas and mosquitoes in the shade,
Celebrate the merger of darkness with midnight, do a dirge
To gods of swamps and hill caves, take three steps forward
Then backward and swerve – left right right left –
Weather changes in circles, dawn ousts darkness . . . Tropical

Summers are hot, but your cell will be a cold, cold winter:
You'll live in that narrow room to the final night.
It's like a piece of thread on which our days hang,
To fall away, one after another, wasted.

ION CARAION (*Romania*)

At The Rotten Sea
....

We shall torture you, we shall kill you and we shall laugh
then we will be killed and others will laugh
we are old enough and shrewd enough
not to care
everything is truth, even the lie
everything is lie, even truth –
darkness begets itself.

Translated by Marguerite Dorian and Elliott B. Urdang

WOLE SOYINKA (*Nigeria*)

After the Deluge
....

Once, for a dare,
He filled his heart-shaped swimming pool
With bank notes, high denomination
And fed a pound of caviar to his dog.
The dog was sick; a chartered plane
Flew in replacement for the Persian rug.

He made a billion yen
Leap from Tokyo to Buenos Aires,
Turn somersaults through Brussels,
New York, Sofia and Johannesburg.
It cracked the bullion market open wide.
Governments fell, coalitions cracked
Insurrection raised its bloody flag
From north to south.

He knew his native land through iron gates,
His sight was radar bowls, his hearing
Electronic beams. For flesh and blood,
Kept company with a brace of Dobermans.
But – yes – the worthy causes never lacked
His widow's mite, discreetly publicised.

He escaped the lynch days. He survives.
I dreamt I saw him on a village
Water line, a parched land where
Water is a god
That doles its favors by the drop,
And waiting is a way of life.
Rebellion gleamed yet faintly in his eye
Traversing chrome-and-platinum retreats. There,
Hubs of commerce smoothly turn without
His bidding, and cities where he lately roosted
Have forgotten him, the preying bird
Of passage.

They let him live, but not from pity
Or human sufferance. He scratches life
From earth, no worse a mortal man than the rest.
Far, far away in dreamland splendor,
Creepers twine his gates of bronze relief.
The jade-lined pool is home
To snakes and lizards; they hunt and mate
On crusted algae.

MBELLA SONNE DIPOKO (*Cameroon*)

Pain

All was quiet in this park
Until the wind, like a gasping messenger, announced
The tyrant's coming
Then did the branches talk in agony.
You remember that raging storm?

In their fear despairing flowers nevertheless held
Bouquets to the grim king;
Meteors were the tassels of his crown
While like branches that only spoke when the storm menaced
We cried in agony as we fell
Slashed by the cold blade of an invisible sword.

Mutilated, our limbs were swept away by the rain;
But not our blood;
Indelible, it stuck on the walls
Like wild gum on tree-trunks.

JAMES K. BAXTER (*New Zealand*)

A Rope for Harry Fat

Oh some have killed in angry love
    And some have killed in hate,
And some have killed in foreign lands
    To serve the business State.
The hangman's hands are abstract hands
    Though sudden death they bring –
"The hangman keeps our country pure,"
    Says Harry Fat the King.

Young love will kick the chairs about
    And like a rush fire burn,
Desiring what it cannot have,
    A true love in return.
Who knows what rage and darkness fall
    When lovers' thoughts turn cold?
"Whoever kills must pay the price,"
    Says Harry Fat the old.

With violent hands a young man tries
    To mend the shape of life.
This one used a shotgun
    And that one used a knife.
And who can see the issues plain
    That vex our groaning dust?
"The law is greater than the man,"
    Says Harry Fat the just.

Te Whiu was too young to vote,
    The prison records show
Some thought he was too young to hang;
    Legality said, *No.*
Who knows what fear the raupo hides
    Or where the wild duck flies?
"A trapdoor and a rope is best,"
    Says Harry Fat the wise.

Though many a time he rolled his coat
	And on the bare boards lay,
He lies in heavy concrete now
	Until the Reckoning Day.
In linen sheet or granite aisle
	Sleep Ministers of State.
"We cannot help the idle poor,"
	Says Harry Fat the great.

Mercy stirred like a summer wind
	The wigs and polished boots
And the long Jehovah faces
	Above their Sunday suits.
The jury was uncertain;
	The judge debated long.
"Let justice take her rightful course,"
	Said Harry Fat the strong.

The butcher boy and baker boy
	Were whistling in the street
When the hangman bound Te Whiu's eyes
	And strapped his hands and feet,
Who stole to buy a bicycle
	And killed in panic blood.
"The parson won his soul at length,"
	Said Harry Fat the good.

Oh some will kill in rage and fear
	And some will kill in hate,
And some will kill in foreign lands
	To serve the master State.
Justice walks heavy in the land;
	She bears a rope and shroud.
"We will not change our policy,"
	Says Harry Fat the proud.

VINCENT BUCKLEY (*Australia*)

Having revised our gods
....

Having revised our gods,
we are intently changing the animals:
re-originating species.
In cold practice rooms the shape-changers
graft fish on flesh, toad on mammal,
mating old enemies, for ever and ever.
We have proved there are no 'natures'. Now
to show there is no Nature. And
'the time is not far off when a human being
can decide not to be, biologically speaking, human.'
Didn't we manage that aeons ago?
And if nature, like god, is just a language,
there'll be lots, mainly the Past, to talk about,
but no names for the new animals.

THOM GUNN (*UK*)

No Speech from the Scaffold

There will be no speech from
the scaffold, the scene must
be its own commentary.

The glossy chipped
surface of the block is like
something for kitchen use.

And the masked man with his
chopper: we know him: he
works in a warehouse nearby.

Last, the prisoner, he
is pale, he walks through
the dewy grass, nodding

a goodbye to acquaintances.
There will be no speech. And we
have forgotten his offence.

What he did is, now,
immaterial. It is the
execution that matters, or,

rather, it is his conduct
as he rests there, while
he is still a human.

STEVIE SMITH (*UK*)

The Death Sentence
....

Cold as No Plea,
Yet wild with all negation,
Weeping I come
To my heart's destination,
To my last bed
Between th'unhallowed boards –
The Law allows it
And the Court awards.

[1950]

R. H. MORRISON (*Australia*)

Black Deaths

We do not hang them now, but still they hang,
though warders' hands are clean as a white sheet.
A little silent air beneath the feet –
no sounds of violence, no cries, no bang.

Nothing accuses more than loss of hope
sprung from the blackness of a black despair:
invisible infection in the air,
one of its symptoms epidemic rope.

A wail goes up beside some camp-fire's embers
where children's eyes and charred food share the flies.
In some far noose another lost one dies,
and one of the surviving lost remembers.

SIPHO SEPAMLA (*South Africa*)

Tell Me News

Tell me of a brother
who hanged himself in prison
with a blanket
was he punch-drunk

Tell me of a brother
who flung himself to death
from the ninth floor of a building
did his grip fumble with the loneliness up there

Tell me of a hooded man
who picked out others of his blood on parade
was his skin beginning
to turn with solitude

Oh, tell me of a sister
who returned home pregnant
from a prison cell
has she been charged under the Immorality Act

Tell me of a brother
who hanged himself in jail
with a piece of his torn pair of jeans
was he hiding a pair of scissors in the cell

Tell me, tell me, sir
has the gruesome sight
of a mangled corpse
not begun to sit on your conscience

VINCENT BUCKLEY (*Australia*)

Internment

They have him squeezed   into the square room
Patrick Shivers   stripped naked   a tight bag
covering his head   feet splayed   rope round his neck
all day   for fourteen hours
fingers tight against the wall   blood hammered back
into his hands   his brain screaming with a noise
as of compressed air   his mouth without water
scum filling his lips

of the right age, Catholic, the right sort,
                    he will stay there
useless as a twig   his shadow
soaking into the floor underneath him

and during this time he began to think of
his son, "The youngster
who had died at six months old"
"I prayed that God would not let me
go insane." "One time
I thought or imagined I had died.
Could not see youngster's face, but felt
reconciled to death. Felt happy."

              And "during this time
              no words spoken at all   bag still
              over my head   I did not speak,
              but prayed out loud.
              Noise going all the time."
              "I tried to speak. Could only whisper
              'Why did you do this to me?'
              Man behind me holding bag pulled me
              said, 'Speak up, I can't hear you.'"

              Patrick Shivers
a mouthful of water after five days.

DENNIS BRUTUS (*South Africa*)

Poems About Prison

....

1

Cold

the clammy cement
sucks our naked feet

a rheumy yellow bulb
lights a damp grey wall

the stubbled grass
wet with three o'clock dew
is black with glittery edges;

we sit on the concrete,
stuff with our fingers
the sugarless pap
into our mouths

then labour erect;

form lines;

steel ourselves into fortitude
or accept an image of ourselves
numb with resigned acceptance;

the grizzled senior warder comments:
"Things like these
I have no time for;

they are worse than rats;
you can only shoot them."

Overhead
the large frosty glitter of the stars
the Southern Cross flowering low;

the chains on our ankles
and wrists
that pair us together
jangle

glitter.

We begin to move
      awkwardly.

(COLESBERG: EN ROUTE TO ROBBEN ISLAND)

NGUYEN CHI THIEN (*Vietnam*)

I Kept Silent

....

I kept silent when I was tortured by my enemy:
With iron and with steel, soul faint in agony –
The heroic stories are for children to believe.
I kept silent because I kept telling myself:
Has anyone, who entered the jungle and who was
      run over by the wild beast
Been stupid enough to open his mouth and ask for mercy?

Translated by Nguyen Huu Hieu

KIM KWANG-SŎP (*North Korea*)

Punishment

···

I, Number 2,223
Draped in the garb of a prisoner
Wearing an alias on my chest
Sitting alone in the North Solitary Confinement Cell
Room 62 Cellblock 3
Of the famous West Gate Penitentiary,
Ask myself,
"Am I Kwangsŏp?"

Three years and eight months
One thousand three-hundred-odd days
Without skipping a single day
Counting the hours on my fingers
With my manure bucket, washstand, and rag
With my chopsticks and enamelware bowl,
I've lived on the plank
In the dark of my fetid room

When summer is long and the days are muggy
I call for the sea and long for the mountains
My mind persistent as scallion *kimch'i*
Sets my tired, pent-up breath afire
And I want to burn, too

Pursued by the cold of long, long winter nights
When my back is cold and bent at the waist
More than sorrow or more than hunger
I felt the hairs on the back of my head, one by one
As though loaded with hoarfrost

Although now I'm living as Kwangsŏp,
Now I don't know what I've lost,
Now I don't know what I've gained and I just exist

However, though I stroll beneath the blue sky,
Suddenly incomprehensible darkness flies at me and
There is nothing more dismal for me than this

So when my eyelids somehow become rheumy
And I don't even know from where the tears are coming,
My tears, now, at last
Belong to fate even more than to love

As reparation for this darkness
With which human rights were trampled and freedom was punished,
Japan, have you withdrawn?
As for me, though you give me your country, I'll spurn it.

Translated by Edward D. Rockstein and Peter H. Lee

JANA ŠTROBLOVÁ (*Czechoslovakia*)

The slaughterhouse

Certainly somewhere there's paradise
where the lamb sleeps curled up with the wolves and a man
buries his face in the lion's mane
but we are so far removed
that the butchers jauntily lash
the calf they're taking for execution
and skin the seals alive

Hold my hand while I tell you this
Pain hurts me I always shut my eyes
when in the cinema something bad
was happening

We shut our eyes
they open the slaughterhouse

Those who don't mind blood

And they trample a daisy a tree
kick a dog
and people
those they can kick
in the groin
The weak

The knife-edge of their denseness detonator of small-
     mindedness
and there is war
started by a bowstring tremor of the veins
by bad children playing the game of blood-flesh-bone

Don't shut your eyes

Hold my hand in this world

Translated by Jarmila and Ian Milner

122

JÁNOS PILINSZKY (*Hungary*)

The Passion

Only the warmth of the slaughter-house,
its geranium pungency, its soft shellac,
only the sun exists.

In a glass-cased silence
the butcher-boys wash down. Yet what has happened
somehow cannot even now finish.

Translated by János Csokits and Ted Hughes

TSUBOI SHIGEJI (*Japan*)

Autumn in gaol

In autumn a friend
Sent in an apple.
I made to eat it
All at once.
Red: too red.

In my palm, heavy:
Heavy as the world.

Translated by Geoffrey Bownas and Anthony Thwaite

MARJORIE AGOSIN (*Chile*)

The most unbelievable part

The most unbelievable part,
they were people like us
good manners
well-educated and refined.
Versed in abstract sciences,
always took a box for the Symphony
made regular trips to the dentist
attended very nice prep schools
some played golf . . .

Yes, people like you, like me
family men
grandfathers
uncles and godfathers.

But they went crazy
delighted in burning
children and books
played at decorating cemeteries
bought furniture made of broken bones
dined on tender ears and testicles.

Thought they were invincible
meticulous in their duties
and spoke of torture
in the language of surgeons and butchers.

They assassinated the young of my country
and of yours.
now nobody could believe in Alice through the looking glass
now nobody could stroll along the avenues
without terror bursting through their bones

And the most unbelievable part
they were people
like you
like me
yes, nice people
just like us.

Translated by Cola Franzen

DENNIS BRUTUS (*South Africa*)

Their Behaviour

Their guilt
is not so very different from ours:
– who has not joyed in the arbitrary exercise of
     power
or grasped for himself what might have been
     another's
and who has not used superior force in the
     moment when he could,
(and who of us has not been tempted to these
     things?) –
so, in their guilt,
the bared ferocity of teeth,
chest-thumping challenge and defiance,
the deafening clamour of their prayers
to a deity made in the image of their prejudice
which drowns the voice of conscience,
is mirrored our predicament
but on a social, massive, organised scale
which magnifies enormously
as the private deshabille of love
becomes obscene in orgies.

(BLOOD RIVER DAY 1965)

GWEN HARWOOD (*Australia*)

Barn Owl

Daybreak: the household slept.
I rose before the sun.
A horny fiend, I crept
out with my father's gun.
Let him dream of a child
obedient, angel-mild –

old No-sayer, robbed of power
by sleep. I knew my prize
who swooped home at this hour
with daylight-riddled eyes
to his place on a high beam
in our old stables, to dream

light's useless time away.
I stood, holding my breath,
in urine-scented hay,
master of life and death,
a wisp-haired judge whose law
would punish beak and claw.

My first shot struck. He swayed,
ruined, beating his only
wing as I watched, afraid
by the fallen gun, a lonely
child who believed death clean
and final, not this obscene

bundle of stuff that dropped
and dribbled through loose straw
tangling its bowels, and hopped
blindly closer. I saw
those eyes that did not see
mirror my cruelty

while the wrecked thing that could
not bear the light nor hide
hobbled in its own blood.
My father reached my side,
gave me the fallen gun.
"End what you have begun."

I fired. The blank eyes shone
once into mine, and slept.
I leaned my head upon
my father's arm, and wept
owl-blind in morning sun
for what I had begun.

JÁNOS PILINSZKY (*Hungary*)

Fable

....

(*Detail from* KZ-Oratorio: Dark Heaven)

Once upon a time
there was a lonely wolf
lonelier than the angels.

He happend to come to a village.
He fell in love with the first house he saw.

Already he loved its walls
the caresses of its bricklayers.
But the window stopped him.

In the room sat people.
Apart from God nobody ever
found them so beautiful
as this child-like beast.

So at night he went into the house.
He stopped in the middle of the room
and never moved from there any more.

He stood all through the night, with wide eyes
and on into the morning when he was beaten to death.

Translated by János Csokits and Ted Hughes

VI

Woman of earth, woman of fire

The difference between Despair
And Fear – is like the One
Between the instant of a Wreck –
And when the Wreck has been –

EMILY DICKINSON

GLORIA DIÉZ (*Spain*)

Woman of Air, Woman of Water

I know that a seaweed wind
obliterated long ago
any trace of my footsteps.
That today's space
makes a place for an image
no more defined than that
hidden in the past.

I do not yet aspire to wrap up
melodious secrets
in the ample folds
of a mystic dress.
I have learned that man
has certain limits.
That the infinite is
hidden in the shadows
thrown by its lights.

I have already abandoned
the air paths,
have allowed water
to soil my skin
with that bitter salt
that impregnates whatever lives.

And now
that I have conquered
because I have been conquered,
I vaguely understand
that my woman of air,
my woman of water,
will be a woman of earth,
a woman of fire.

Translated by J.C.R. Green, Albert Rowe and Sandra MacGregor Hastie

Irina Ratushinskaya (*USSR*)

Give me a nickname, prison

Give me a nickname, prison,
this first April
evening of sadness
shared with you.
This hour for your songs
of evil and goodness,
confessions of love,
salty jokes.
They've taken my friends,
ripped the cross from its chain,
torn clothes,
and then with boots
struck at my breastbone
torturing the remains
of hope.
My name is filed
in profile, full-face –
a numbered dossier.
In custody –
nothing is mine!
Just as you have
no one, nothing!
On the window's grating
here's all of me – christen me,
give me a name, prison,
send off to the transport
not a boy, but a zek,
so I'll be welcomed
with endearments by Kolyma,
place of outcasts, executions
in this twentieth century.

[5 OCTOBER 1983]

Translated by Frances Padorr Brent and Carol J. Avins

DAVID CONSTANTINE (*UK*)

Poem on my birthday for Irina Ratushinskaya

We have the day in common, also verses;
And the cold has lasted beyond what is usual;
By now there should be coltsfoot. Cold?
It hurts the face a little, the eyes weep perhaps,
But you should see my son brake his toboggan broadside,
You should kiss my bright-eyed daughter cycled home.

Some things are black and white: laws against poems,
A camp on the driven snow. Do the guards enquire
Through the eyes of the line of unspeaking women
Who harbours your verses now? I have read of such cold
That the breath you breathe makes a starry whisper,
It forms on the air, it crackles like interference.

What have you done? They can question you to death,
They can feed your lungs with ice, they can dose
The freely riding waves of the air with dust.
You imprinted the dirty glass with frost gardens,
You muttered of love along the nissen corridors.
Oh triumph of breath! Oh manifest beauty of breathing!

Just now in the dark, turning a year older,
I heard the rain begin. Soon in our country
The little horns of lilac will butt at the sky.
Our house warms through its pipes. The whisper of rain,
A continuous whispering of verses. Courage,
Sister. Good courage, my white sister.

[4 MARCH 1986]

ES'KIA MPHAHLELE (*South Africa*)

Somewhere

....

Somewhere a mother sobs
through bomb-shattered nights
hunger drains the blood of children.
Somewhere we eat the sputum of our pride
when we know nothing and we blunder.
Somewhere a woman sees her sick man
teeter on the edge of midnight
and turn his back to her and all forever.
Somewhere in the arena we lose our head
amid the boos and jeers and whoops
along the sidelines.
Somewhere a mother awaits
her man, her son
in chains of an oppressor
or waits for those who never come
and still endures we know not how.
And yet amid the smoking debris
of a fear-driven world
while man juggles with megaton eggs,
somewhere a woman gives the world an artist:
a child who sings and dances,
dreams and weaves a poem round the universe
plunging down the womb
to fire a cell
sinking down a borehole
to probe the spring of life
from where the earth will rise
to meet the sky.
Somewhere in ancient China, it is told,
a man made a song
out of the wailing of a dove
a song that moved all animals
to rise and kill the serpent
who ate the bird's young ones.
To know our sorrow
is to know our joy –
Somewhere a mother will rejoice.

EDILBERTO COUTINHO (*Brazil*)

The fight goes on

FIRST HALF

She serves him coffee with a tiny, delicate hand.

So nervous, she says to the man, because they told her: be prepared for the worst.

The only thought in her mind the past few weeks: her boy's disappearance.

They're simply picking up everyone for no reason at all, aren't they?

That's right. You've no need to worry.

The man in the orange shirt and check trousers, slender, soft-spoken, suddenly says:

Tomorrow the sun will shine.

Ah, she says, thanks so much. But tell me, aren't you frightened?

People only die once, the man says. Then: That was a great cup of coffee.

Like another?

No, thanks all the same.

Now she trusts him.

Is my boy in jail? Tell me the truth. Has something awful happened?

Everything's all right, don't worry.

Don't upset yourself. He asked us to tell you. He's gone away. So he won't be in touch for a while. He wants me to send some things on to him. Things he left in his room. In the drawers of his wardrobe. Could you show me? The mother leads the stranger to the room. He starts to rummage. One drawer, then another, another. Searching through papers. Finds something.

Says goodbye:

Thank you ever so much.

God be with you. When will I see him?

Beg pardon?

My son.

Soon, I hope.

SECOND HALF

But I only took him to your room after he said the password.

I know, mother. Don't worry, the fight goes on. Don't upset yourself about it.

I'm terrified. Aren't you?

People only die once, the boy says.

Will they at least let you eat the banana cake?

Sure they will.

How are they treating you?

Fine.

They were talking standing up. His legs were aching, so he sat down. Absent-mindedly, he pulled up his trouser legs, for a bit of air. Hot? Stifling. She saw:

What are those marks? Have you got them all over your body?

Don't worry, mother.

He insisted: They treat me fine. They'll let me eat the banana cake.

It was such a pleasure baking it for you.

A.D. HOPE (*Australia*)

Massacre of the Innocents

(*After Cornelis van Haarlem*)

The big sweet muscles of an athlete's dream
Pose for the sporting picture; Herod's guard
Opposes the selected Ladies' Team.
The game is Murder, played as a charade.

The white meat of the woman, prime and sleek,
Fends off the bull male from her squealing spawn;
The tenderloin, the buttock's creamy cheek,
Against the gladiator's marble brawn.

This is the classic painter's butcher shop;
– Choice cuts from the Antique – Triumphant Mars
Takes his revenge, the whistling falchions swoop
Round Venus as the type of all mammas.

The game is Nightmare: now, in the grotesque
Abortion of his love-dream, she displays
The pale, ripe carcass of the odalisque,
Now the brood-female in her mastoid grace.

The unruptured egg shrieks in her fallow womb.
Freckled with blood his knife-arm plunges straight
For the fat suckling's throat. He drives it home
Full loaded with his contraceptive hate.

OSIP MANDELSTAM (*USSR*)

Through Kiev

Through Kiev, through the streets of the monster
some wife's trying to find her husband.
One time we knew that wife,
the wax cheeks, dry eyes.

Gypsies won't tell fortunes for beauties.
Here the concert hall has forgotten the instruments.
Dead horses along the main street.
The morgue smells in the nice part of town.

The Red Army trundled its wounded
out of town on the last street car,
one blood-stained overcoat calling,
"Don't worry, we'll be back!"

[VORONEZH, MAY 1937]

Translated by Clarence Brown and W.S. Merwin

ELAINE FEINSTEIN (*UK*)

Offering: for Marina Tsvetayeva

Through yellow fingers smoke rises about you
now we enter your transfigured life
what were those recoveries
of hope you kept to
starved ferocious ill
poet rough-clothed and cold-fingered
pushed more than loss of
lovers or even a dead child over
the edge of blackness in middle age.
When you went back to Russia   to
Efron your gentle husband   a
murderer   soon murdered   was it
in loneliness   the ear and
tongue of a language you looked for?
As misery closed in, with a last
hatred   had you
abandoned that strange trust
even when you hung yourself coldly like
an unwanted dog? O black icon.

ANNA AKHMATOVA (*USSR*)

Crucifixion

....

"Mother, do not weep for Me,
who am in the grave."

I

Angelic choirs the unequalled hour exalted,
And heaven disintegrated into flame.
Unto the Father: "Why hast Thou forsaken . . .!"
But to the Mother: "Do not weep for me . . ."

II

Magdalina beat her breast and wept, while
The loved disciple seemed hammered out of stone.
But, for the Mother, where she stood in silence, –
No one as much as dared to look that way.

Translated by D.M. Thomas

R.F. BRISSENDEN (*Australia*)

The Death of Damiens or
l'Après-midi des lumières

Place de Grève, Paris, March 28, 1757

The man's left leg
Is torn away at last.
It drags behind the stallion
Over the cobbles.

The waiting crowd
Packed like cattle into the square
Clap, roar and stamp their feet.
The man kisses the crucifix.

From a high window
Casanova and his friend,
Six-times-a-night Tiretta,
Watch with their women.

Immaculate in white,
Henri Sanson with glowing pincers
Plucks out a lump of flesh
From the man's bared chest.

His five assistant executioners
Moving like priests
Pour in the boiling oil,
The molten lead.

The stench fills the square.
The lathered horses,
Jerking under the whip,
Strain at the heavy cables.

Tiretta, unbuttoned,
Lifts from behind the long silk skirt
Of the Pope's niece.
The other leg comes off.

Robert Damiens screams.
Casanova, cupping the warm young breast
Of Mademoiselle de la Meure,
Turns her virginal head away.

"Animals, animals!" he mutters
Smiling. "Look, my dear
The dying madman's hair
Has all gone white."

ROSS CLARK (*Australia*)

Spoils to the Victors

Always, when the conquerors come
with their strange urgent tongues,
it is the women who know what they say.

It is the women who know the language
of the tongue in the head, and the angrier
tongue in the hips that compels its

bitter alphabet to be uttered
in every conquered household.

CHRISTINE LAVANT (*Austria*)

Fear has risen in me

Fear has risen in me.
Like a woman who suddenly remembers something terrible
and who then – if she has two rooms –
walks from one to the other,
that's how fear is walking in me now.
Often I talk to her,
sing to her and pray for her,
or I read to her for hours
from books that are very wise, very sacred.
She doesn't care.
She only grows heavier
until every spot she stands on
begins to tremble.
So everything in me trembles too,
knees, hands and lips
and my eyelids probably most of all.
But she cannot rest
and through the door of my mind
breaks into my poor soul.
There, too, everything is wavering.
Images of heaven and hell
tumble over each other and over her, the fear.
Oh, poor woman!
She will never find sleep,
she will never let me sleep:
someone gave her a word
which hangs like a sword
on the thread of a single hope
above us.

Translated by Andrew Taylor and Beate Josephi

IVA KOTRLA (*Czechoslovakia*)

Growing Up

In the years
when the secret police
took down our faces
    as we left the church
we reached out
    into our dreams

Every evening
adulthood came, with a lamp,
to our bedside,
    quietly drew aside the curtains
and spoke to us
    gently, like a mother.

Translated by Josef Skvorecky

MARJORIE AGOSIN (*Chile*)

The God of Children

....

– For Elena Gascón-Vera

They undressed her and bound her
and speaking precisely as diplomats and surgeons
asked her
which God she believed in
that of the Moors or that of the Jews
head hanging and so far away
she kept saying
I believe in the God of children.

Translated by Cola Franzen

MARY GILMORE (*Australia*)

Nationality

....

I have grown past hate and bitterness,
I see the world as one;
But though I can no longer hate,
My son is still my son.

All men at God's round table sit,
And all men must be fed;
But this loaf in my hand,
This loaf is my son's bread.

MAXINE KUMIN (*USA*)

The Envelope

It is true, Martin Heidegger, as you have written,
I fear to cease, even knowing that the hour
of my death my daughters will absorb me, even
knowing they will carry me about forever
inside them, an arrested fetus, even as I carry
the ghost of my mother under my navel, a nervy
little androgynous person, a miracle
folded in lotus position.

Like those old pear-shaped Russian dolls that open
at the middle to reveal another and another, down
to the pea-sized, irreducible minim,
may we carry our mothers forth in our bellies.
May we, borne onward by our daughters, ride
in the Envelope of Almost-Infinity,
that chain letter good for the next twenty-five
thousand days of their lives.

146

VII

....

Their embassies, he said, were everywhere

For who is
the judge, and what is the judgment,
unless it be in the full sense of the night
and in the full severity of mercy.

YEHUDA AMICHAI

LES MURRAY (*Australia*)

An Absolutely Ordinary Rainbow

The word goes round Repins, the murmur goes round Lorenzinis,
At Tattersalls, men look up from sheets of numbers,
The Stock Exchange scribblers forget the chalk in their hands
And men with bread in their pockets leave the Greek Club:
There's a fellow crying in Martin Place. They can't stop him.

The traffic in George Street is banked up for half a mile
And drained of motion. The crowds are edgy with talk
And more crowds come hurrying. Many run in the back streets
Which minutes ago were busy main streets, pointing:
There's a fellow weeping down there. No one can stop him.

The man we surround, the man no one approaches
Simply weeps, and does not cover it, weeps
Not like a child, not like the wind, like a man
And does not declaim it, nor beat his breast, nor even
Sob very loudly – yet the dignity of his weeping

Holds us back from his space, the hollow he makes about him
In the midday light, in his pentagram of sorrow,
And uniforms back in the crowd who tried to seize him
Stare out at him, and feel, with amazement, their minds
Longing for tears as children for a rainbow.

Some will say, in the years to come, a halo
Or force stood around him. There is no such thing.
Some will say they were shocked and would have stopped him
But they will not have been there. The fiercest manhood,
The toughest reserve, the slickest wit amongst us

Trembles with silence, and burns with unexpected
Judgements of peace. Some in the concourse scream
Who thought themselves happy. Only the smallest children
And such as look out of Paradise come near him
And sit at his feet, with dogs and dusty pigeons.

Ridiculous, says a man near me, and stops
His mouth with his hands, as if it uttered vomit –
And I see a woman, shining, stretch her hand
And shake as she receives the gift of weeping;
As many as follow her also receive it

And many weep for sheer acceptance, and more
Refuse to weep for fear of all acceptance,
But the weeping man, like the earth, requires nothing,
The man who weeps ignores us, and cries out
Of his writhen face and ordinary body

Not words, but grief, not messages, but sorrow
Hard as the earth, sheer, present as the sea –
And when he stops, he simply walks between us
Mopping his face with the dignity of one
Man who has wept, and now has finished weeping.

Evading believers, he hurries off down Pitt Street.

TED HUGHES (*UK*)

How Water Began to Play

Water wanted to live
It went to the sun it came weeping back
Water wanted to live
It went to the trees they burned it came weeping back
They rotted it came weeping back
Water wanted to live
It went to the flowers they crumpled it came weeping back
It wanted to live
It went to the womb it met blood
It came weeping back
It went to the womb it met knife
It came weeping back
It went to the womb it met maggot and rottenness
It came weeping back it wanted to die

It went to time it went through the stone door
It came weeping back

It went searching through all space for nothingness
It came weeping back it wanted to die

Till it had no weeping left

It lay at the bottom of all things

Utterly worn out   utterly clear.

ALLEN AFTERMAN (*USA*)

Pietà

....

I leave it for you to say why it is
that every moment we are awake we do not weep?
How is it we walk the streets
and do not fall on our knees before anyone
who is still beautiful, or who is ugly?
I think of those pyramids in sealed chambers;
of those sealed in ghettos
who ate the arms of their children, dead in frozen urine.
Would you picture this with me?

      How is it we are able to forget them;
that we dare to have other than those children?

I think of the mute, black children
their mothers held by the scruff of the neck
for the minutes it took . . .

Why is it
we do not memorise each name, every word whispered,
the texture of the ground, the colour of the clouds,
the executioner's gestures . . .

Why is it that every moment we are awake we do not weep?

Irina Ratushinskaya (*USSR*)

We will not go into that river

We will not go into that river
not part the overgrown banks,
for us, there will never be a lame man
prepared to take us across.

But there will be an evening – warm, like an infusion
of warm grasses; lassitude and silence.
Then the prison camp cot will retract
and the cell's coldness, draft from the window.

We'll remember conversation through walls,
happiest dreams in half-delirium.
Mordovian peasant-women, passing us crusts of bread:
– *At least take a bite, don't go hungry!*

And this is for us to bring our loved ones,
honestly dividing – what for whom:
all that terrifies – to ourselves,
all evil – past us,
all goodness of the earth – for his shoulder.

[16 FEBRUARY 1984]

Translated by Frances Padorr Brent and Carol J. Avins

DENNIS BRUTUS (*South Africa*)

Somehow We Survive

Somehow we survive
and tenderness, frustrated, does not wither.

Investigating searchlights rake
our naked unprotected contours;

over our heads the monolithic decalogue
of fascist prohibition glowers
and teeters for a catastrophic fall;

boots club on the peeling door.

But somehow we survive
severance, deprivation, loss.

Patrols uncoil along the asphalt dark
hissing their menace to our lives;

most cruel, all our land is scarred with terror,
rendered unlovely and unlovable;
sundered are we and all our passionate surrender

but somehow tenderness survives.

JANET FRAME (*New Zealand*)

When the Sun Shines More Years Than Fear

When the sun shines more years than fear
when birds fly more miles than anger
when sky holds more bird
sails more cloud
shines more sun
than the palm of love carries hate,
even then shall I in this weary
seventy-year banquet say, Sunwaiter,
Birdwaiter, Skywaiter,
I have no hunger,
remove my plate.

SHAO YANXIANG (*China*)

I'll Always Remember
....

Thirty-three tribunals of public censure
Thirty-three bold-character posters
Thirty-three waves and thirty-three storms
Thirty-three tramplings underfoot . . .
Simply because you
Cast me a secretive glance
That would wipe away
Grief from the sky and sorrow from my heart

Sixty-six shout-downs and harassments
Sixty-six floggings and beatings
Sixty-six dismemberments and humiliations
Sixty-six torture sessions and strangulations . . .
I heard voiceless language
From your closed lips
Telling me in the dead of winter
That flowers somewhere hadn't all withered

Ninety-nine cursings
Ninety-nine wounds
Ninety-nine death sentences
Ninety-nine levels of hell . . .
Could not have overcome
Your hand stretched forth to prop me –
That wisp of tenderness
Rescued me a hundred times a hundred times

I'll always remember your bitter smile
You'll always remember my pained loyalty
Belief
Ah, my belief
Let's cast a contemptuous look
On those whose stratagems all came to naught

[18 MARCH 1981]

Translated by Fang Dai, Dennis Ding and Edward Morin

SHAO YANXIANG (*China*)

My Optimism

I'm an adult
My optimism is adult too

My optimism
Doesn't smile all the time
It has rolled in the mud
It's been struck on an anvil
It burst out into sparks under the hammer
It burned in a bonfire that almost went out
For a while people scornfully called it dead ash

It has been worked over with nightsticks
Jerked around every which way,
Then floated downriver chilled to the bone
None of its fibres
Is tainted by even a speck of dust
It doesn't wear coveralls
Not my optimism

My optimism
Isn't a coat
That you sometimes put on and then take off
Nor does it have a pocket with a conscience inside
That you could sometimes bring with you
Or sometimes leave at home

My optimism
Leaped into my arms
And I warmed it up with my body heat
After it had been trampled when those
Who had once embraced it cast it aside

I warmed it up
And it warmed me
Double-crossed
And reported on in secret

It grew up step by step
Yet without encountering obstacles
Without a taste of mean tricks
How could my optimism become adult?

Adult optimism
Isn't always sweet
Sometimes its face is bathed in tears
I once heard it choking back sobs
But it woke out of its grief
Caught my hand
Comforted my heart
Propped my head in both hands
And tried gently to console me
With a tune that only parents would use for a child
Hello old friend inseparable as body and shadow
My long-suffering weather-beaten optimism

[28 JANUARY 1984]

Translated by Fang Dai, Dennis Ding and Edward Morin

BRUCE DAWE (*Australia*)

Description of an Idea

You can nail it to a cross
and it will rise again after three days.
You can put it in the arena with several wild beasts
and it will survive its own dismemberment.
You can tie it to a stake and light faggots under it
and the crackling of the flames will speak volumes.
You can exile it to Siberia
and it will still cry out with the voice of Ivan Denisovich.
You can beat it to a bloody pulp in a public square in
    Peking
and it will still think of freedom.
You can turn the Star Chamber and the SS
      and the KGB and the Savak
         and the State Security Bureau
            loose on it
and someone somewhere will still think it
and someone somewhere will still die for it
and someone somewhere will give it new life.
For an idea is an organism more mysterious in its action
than the miracidium.
. . . You can declare an idea anathema to 999,999,999 people
and the billionth will reach for a dictionary . . .

SHERKO BEKAS (*Iraq*)

In a forest

Darkness came
And in its lair, a lion thought
Of how, tomorrow, to attack the neighbouring tiger.
The tiger was thinking:
Of how, tomorrow, to skin the fox.
The fox was thinking:
Of how, tomorrow, to approach the
    garden's gate to eat
    the baby-doves.
The dove was thinking:
Of how, tomorrow, to bring together
    the hunter, the birds and
    the animals of the forest.
How could she, she wondered.

Translated by Hussain Sinjari

GWEN HARWOOD (*Australia*)

Morning Again

Morning again, though not yet light.
The next-door bantams call me up
in a strange world where dream and waking
melt in a featureless expanse.

Some time of violence has been close.
No relics mark that endless plain,
but someone's buried, some new ghost
between one cockcrow and the next

is fretting. Now a figure rises
so distant one can only tell
from its stretched arms it might be human,
and, close behind, another presence

not human marks its stumbling flight;
cloudy enough to blur the line
of any possible horizon
yet like enough to all I fear

for me to know I am the human
figure with aching arms extended,
casting no shadow, reaching out
for substance in my flight from terror.

Safety: calm light on leaf and feather.
Here is the news. And now, the weather –
an ordinary human shadow
attends me as I fill the kettle.

FAIZ AHMAD FAIZ (*Pakistan*)

A Prison Nightfall

The night descends
step by silent step
down the stairway of stars.
The breeze goes by me
like a kindly whispered phrase.

The homeless trees of the prison yard
are absorbed, making patterns
against the sky.

On the roof's high crest
the loving hand of moonlight rests.
The starry river is drowned in dust
and the sky glows silver with moonlight.
In the dark foliage
shadows play with the wind
as a wave of painful loss
invades the heart.

Defiantly, a thought tells me
how sweet life is at this instant:
Those who brew the poison of cruelty
will not win, tomorrow or today.
They can put out the lamps
where lovers meet;
they cannot blind the moon!

Translated by Mahmood Jamal

GIUSEPPE UNGARETTI (*Italy*)

Fine Night

What song has risen tonight
to weave
the crystal echo of the heart
with the stars

What honeymoon has sprung
out of my heart

I have been
a pool of darkness

Now
Like a child at his mother's breast
I fasten myself to this night

Now I am drunk
with everything that is

Translated by Kevin Hart

PEGGY SHUMAKER (*USA*)

* Blue Corn, Black Mesa

Before you go, I need to tell you
why here tongues turn dry as piki bread.
No one knows why this story is true

but I know there was a woman who
buried both hands in blue dough. She said,
Before you go, I need to tell you

why Hopi corn grows short, in a few
spindly clumps, not deep and wide and red.
No one knows why this story is true,

but I know it is not a lie. New
seed lay still; the sheep we gave for dead.
Before you go I need to tell you

that crater's spirit gave us breath. Blue
winds swept ash from the mesa, it bled –
no one knows why this story is true –

earth's sky blood washed ragged furrows. Blue
corn cracked, tucked sharp in this lava bed.
Before you go, I need to tell you:
no one knows why this story is true.

---

* Hopi blue corn is a biological riddle. It germinates only in thin volcanic
soil and thrives in the severe, unforgiving climate of the high desert.

PABLO NERUDA (*Chile*)

Nothing More

I stood by truth:
to establish light in the land.

I wanted to be common like bread;
so when the struggle came she wouldn't find me missing.

But here I am with what I loved,
with the solitude I lost:
but by this stone I don't rest.

The sea works in my silence.

Translated by Dennis Maloney

HABIB JALIB (*Pakistan*)

My Daughter

Thinking that it was a toy,
when she saw the chain around my wrists
my daughter jumped for joy.
Her laughter was the gift of morning,
her laughter gave me endless strength.
A living hint of a free tomorrow
gave meaning to my night of sorrow.

Translated by Mahmood Jamal

TOMAS TRANSTRÖMER (*Sweden*)

Open and Closed Rooms

A man touches the world with his trade for a glove.
He rests in the middle of the day leaving his gloves
                        on the shelf.
They suddenly start to grow, inflate themselves
and darken the whole house from the inside.

The darkened house sits surrounded by soft spring winds,
"Amnesty," is the whisper of the grass: "Amnesty."
A boy runs with an invisible string that slants
                        right up into heaven
where his wild dream of the future soars, a kite
                        bigger than the suburb.

Farther north, seen from the hilltop, is an endless blue
                        sprucewood carpet
where the shadows of clouds
stand still.
No, *fly on.*

Translated by May Swenson

EVAN JONES (*Australia*)

The Point

The point, I imagine, is
not to learn to expect
betrayal, self-deceit, lies
however thick they collect
in the cul-de-sac of one's days,
half-noticed, half-numbered, half-checked:
but rather to learn to praise
fidelity, trust and love
which in their modest ways
continue to be and move
(however mocked, however derided,
however difficult, indeed, to prove),
utterly undivided –
if inarticulate or mute,
still mortally decided.

Neither fashionable nor astute
this point to take to heart:
merely final and absolute:

without it no people, no life, no art.

NIYI OSUNDARE (*Nigeria*)

I Sing of Change

....

Sing on: somewhere, at some new moon,
We'll learn that sleeping is not death,
Hearing the whole earth change its tune.
                                    W.B. YEATS

I sing
of the beauty of Athens
without its slaves

Of a world free
of kings and queens
and other remnants
of an arbitrary past

Of earth
with no
sharp north
or deep south
without blind curtains
or iron walls

of the end
of warlords and armouries
and prisons of hate and fear

Of deserts treeing
and fruiting
after the quickening rains

Of the sun
radiating ignorance
and stars informing
nights of unknowing

I sing of a world reshaped

CIRCE MAIA (*Uruguay*)

A Wind Will Come from the South

A wind will come from the south with unleashed rain
to beat on closed doors and on the windows
to beat on faces with bitter expressions.

Happy noisy waves will come
climbing paths and silent streets
through the port district.

Let the hardened city wash its face
its stones and dusty wood, worn out
its heart sombre.

Let there be surprise at least in the opaque
taciturn glances.
And let many people be frightened, and the children laugh
and the greenness of the water's light wake us
bathe us, follow us.

Let it make us run and embrace each other
and let the doors of all the houses open
and the people come out
down the stairs, from the balconies,
calling to each other . . .

Translated by Patsy Boyer and Mary Crow

IRINA RATUSHINSKAYA (*USSR*)

Wildstrawberry Town

In Wildstrawberry Town –
clear-ringing little windows,
in Wildstrawberry Town –
milk for the cat,
in Wildstrawberry Town –
gingerbread with pictures,
towers with clocks,
gypsies with baskets,
puddles and boats,
figs and bananas,
haughty crows,
wise lambs.
All evening – cartoons,
all day – ice cream,
and on Sundays –
second helpings!
They've even recorded
in Wildstrawberry Town –
expressions of happiness
on the face of a horse!
Hedgehogs too,
tigers and bears!
Let's buy heaps of sugar –
set off without cares
to Wildstrawberry Town.

Translated by Frances Padorr Brent and Carol J. Avins

SEAMUS HEANEY (*Ireland*)

From the Republic of Conscience

···

I

When I landed in the republic of conscience
it was so noiseless when the engines stopped
I could hear a curlew high above the runway.

At immigration the clerk was an old man
who produced a wallet from his homespun coat
and showed me a photograph of my grandfather.

The woman in customs asked me to declare
the words of our traditional cures and charms
to heal dumbness and avert the evil eye.

No porter. No interpreter. No taxi.
You carried what you had to and very soon
your symptoms of creeping privilege disappeared.

II

Fog is a dreaded omen there but lightning
spells universal good and parents hang
swaddled infants in trees during thunderstorms.

Salt is their precious mineral. And seashells
are held to the ear during births and funerals.
The base of all inks and pigments is seawater.

Their sacred symbol is a stylised boat.
The sail is an ear, the mast a sloping pen,
the hull a mouth-shape, the keel an open eye.

At their inauguration, public leaders
must swear to uphold unwritten law and weep
to atone for their presumption to hold office –

170

and to affirm their faith that all life sprang
from salt in tears which the sky-god wept
after he dreamt his solitude was endless.

III

I came back from that frugal republic
with my two arms the one length, the customs woman
having insisted my allowance was myself.

The old man rose and gazed into my face
and said that was official recognition
that I was now a dual citizen.

He therefore desired me when I got home
to consider myself a representative
and to speak on their behalf in my own tongue.

Their embassies, he said, were everywhere
but operated independently
and no ambassador would ever be relieved.

Source acknowledgements

The editors and publishers wish to thank all those who have given permission to use copyright material. Thanks also go to the many copyright-holders who expressed encouragement for this international project for Amnesty.

◆ **A** ◆ **Jonathan Aaron** for 'Finding the Landscape' from *Second Sight* (Harper Colophon Books, 1982) © Jonathan Aaron (1982); **Robert Adamson** for 'Canticle For The Bicentennial Dead' from *The Clean Dark* (Paper Bark Press, 1989) © Robert Adamson (1989); Collins Angus & Robertson for **Allen Afterman**'s 'Pietà' from *Purple Adam* (1980) © Allen Afterman (1980); White Pine Press for **Marjorie Agosin**'s 'Disappeared Woman 1', 'The God of Children' and 'The most unbelievable part' from *Zones of Pain* translated by Cola Franzen (1988) © Marjorie Agosin (1988) translations © Cola Franzen (1988); Martin Secker & Warburg for **Anna Akhmatova**'s: 'Behind the lake the moon's not stirred', 'Crucifixion', 'Prologue', 'Why is our century worse than any other?' from *You Will Hear Thunder* translated by D.M. Thomas (1985) translation © D.M. Thomas, 1976, 1979, 1985; University of Pittsburgh Press for **Claribel Alegría**'s 'Little Cambray Tamales' from *Woman of the River*, by Claribel Alegría, translated by D.J. Flakoll (1989) © Claribel Alegría (1989); Penguin Books for **Muhammad Al-Maghut**'s 'The Postman's Fear' from *Modern Poetry of the Arab World*, translated and edited by Abdullah al-Udhari (1986) © Abdullah al-Udhari (1986); **Yehuda Amichai** for 'Of Three or Four in a Room' from *Yehuda Amichai: Selected Poems* edited and translated by Chana Bloch and Stephen Mitchell (Penguin Books, 1988) English translation Chana Bloch and Stephen Mitchell (1986); Faber & Faber and Random House for **W.H. Auden**'s 'Musée des Beaux Arts' from *W.H. Auden: Collected Poems* edited by Edward Mendelson, © W.H. Auden (1940 and 1968).

◆ **B** ◆ Oxford University Press for **James K. Baxter**'s 'A Rope for Harry Fat' from *The Collected Poems of James K. Baxter* edited by J.W. Weir (1980) © Mrs J.C. Baxter; Charles Simic for **Matija Bećković**'s 'If I knew I'd bear myself proudly' from *Contemporary Yugoslav Poetry* edited by Vasa Mihailovich (University of Iowa Press, 1977) © The University of Iowa (1977); *Index on Censorship* for **Sherko Bekas**' 'In a Forest'; Carl Hanser Verlag for **Horst Bienek**'s: 'The Myth of Time', 'Vorkuta' from Gleiwitzer kindheit. Gedichte Aus 20 Jahren. München Wien 1976. English translation by Matthew and Ruth Mead, in *Penguin Modern European Poets* (1971) © Matthew Mead (1969); Farrar, Straus & Giroux, for **Elizabeth Bishop**'s 'The Man-Moth' from *The Complete Poems 1927-1979* (1979, 1983) © Alice Helen Methfessel (1979, 1983); **Rosalind Brackenbury** for 'Looking for Words' from *Telling Each Other It Is Possible* (Taxus Press, 1987) © Rosalind Brackenbury (1987); Rosemary Brissenden for **R.F. Brissenden**'s 'The Death of Damiens, or *l'Après-midi des lumières*' from *The Whale in Darkness* (Australian National University Press, 1980); **Dennis Brutus** for 'Somehow We Survive' and 'The Sounds Begin Again' from *Sirens, Knuckles, Boots* (Mbari Publishing/Northwestern University Press, 1963) © Dennis Brutus (1963) and *A Simple Lust: Selected Poems* (Hill & Wang, 1973) © Dennis Brutus (1973); Heinemann Publishers (Oxford) for **Dennis Brutus**' 'Poems About Prison' and 'Their Behaviour' from *Letters to Martha and Other Poems from a South African Prison* (1968) © Dennis Brutus (1968); Penelope Buckley for **Vincent Buckley**'s 'Having revised our gods' from *Last Poems* (McPhee Gribble, 1991) copyright © Penelope Buckley (1991) and 'Internment' from *The Pattern* (Dolmen Press, 1979) © Estate of Vincent Buckley.

◆ **C** ◆ Ohio University Press for **Ion Caraion**'s 'At the Rotten Sea' from *Ion Caraion: Poems* translated by Marguerite Dorian and Elliott B. Urdang (1981) translations ©

1972); Faber & Faber for **Ted Hughes**' 'How water began to play' from *Crow* **(1972)** © **Ted Hughes (1970, 1972)**.

◆ **J** ◆ Mahmood Jamal for **Habib Jalib**'s 'My Daughter' from *The Penguin Book of Modern Urdu Poetry* selected and translated by Mahmood Jamal (1986) © Mahmood Jamal (1986); **Evan Jones** for 'The Point' from *Recognitions* (ANU Press, 1978) © Evan Jones (1978).

◆ **K** ◆ Kevin Gilbert for **Grandfather Koori**'s 'Massacre Sandhill' from *Inside Black Australia. An Anthology of Aboriginal Poetry* edited by Kevin Gilbert (Penguin Books Australia, 1988) collection © Kevin Gilbert (1988); **Iva Kotrl**a for 'Growing Up'; **Ivan Kraus** for 'The Censor'; Viking Penguin for **Maxine Kumin**'s 'The Envelope' from *Our Ground Time Here Will Be Brief* © Maxine Kumin 1957-1965, 1970-1982; The University of Hawaii Press for **Kim Kwang-söp**'s 'Punishment' translated by Edward D. Rockstein and Peter H. Lee from *The Silence of Love. Twentieth Century Korean Poetry* edited by Peter H. Lee (1980) © The University Press of Hawaii (1980).

◆ **L** ◆ Andrew Taylor and Beate Josephi for **Christine Lavant**'s 'Fear has risen in me' from *Miracles of Disbelief* translated by Andrew Taylor and Beate Josephi (The Leros Press, 1985) © The Leros Press (1985); The University of Hawaii Press for **Liang Xiaobin**'s 'The Snow-White Wall' from *The Red Azalea. Chinese Poetry since the Cultural Revolution* edited by Edward Morin and translated by Fang Dai, Dennis Ding and Edward Morin (1990) © University of Hawaii Press (1990).

◆ **M** ◆ Latin American Literary Review Press for **Circe Maia**'s 'A Wind Will Come from the South' from *Woman Who Has Sprouted Wings* edited by Mary Crow (1984) English translation © Latin American Literary Review Press (1984); Vasa Mihailovich for **Desanka Maksimović**'s 'Now it is certain' translated by Vasa Mihailovich from *Contemporary Yugoslav Poetry* edited by Vasa Mihailovich (University of Iowa Press, 1977) © The University of Iowa (1977); Oxford University Press for **Osip Mandelstam**'s 'Maybe this is the beginning of madness', 'The Stalin Epigram', 'Through Kiev', 'You took away all the oceans' from *Osip Mandelstam: Selected Poems* translated by Clarence Brown and W.S. Merwin (1973) Clarence Brown and W.S. Merwin (1973); Collins Angus & Robertson for **James McAuley**'s 'Jindyworobaksheesh' from *Collected Poems 1936-1970* (1971) © Norma McAuley (1971); Georges Borchardt for **W.S. Merwin**'s 'Some Last Questions' from *The Lice* (Atheneum, 1967) © W.S. Merwin 1963, 1964, 1965, 1966, 1967; Doubleday for **Czeslaw Milosz**' 'Dedication' from *Postwar Polish Poetry* (University of California Press, 1983) © Czeslaw Milosz 1965, 1983; Curbstone Press for **Miguel Huezo Mixco**'s 'If Death ...' from *On the Front Line: Guerrilla Poems of El Salvador* edited and translated by Claribel Alegría and Darwin J. Flakoll (1989) translation © Claribel Alegría and Darwin J. Flakoll (1989); **R.H. Morrison** and *Overland* for 'Black Deaths'; **Es'kia Mphahlele** for 'Somewhere' from *The Unbroken Song*, Ravan Press, 1979; University Press of New England for **Lupenga Mphande**'s 'Song of a Prison Guard' from *When My Brothers Come Home: Poems From Central and South Africa* edited by Frank Chipasula (Wesleyan University Press, 1985) © Frank Chipasula (1985); Oxford University Press for **Mbuyiseni Oswald Mtshali**'s 'Nightfall in Soweto' from *Sounds of a Cowhide Drum* © Mbuyiseni Oswald Mtshali (1971); **Les Murray** for 'An Absolutely Ordinary Rainbow' from *Poems 1961-1983* (Angus & Robertson, 1988) © Les Murray (1983).

◆ **N** ◆ Mahmood Jamal for **Kishwar Naheed**'s 'Listen To Me' from *The Penguin Book of Modern Urdu Poetry* selected and translated by Mahmood Naheed (1986) © Mahmood Naheed (1986); Dennis Maloney for **Pablo Neruda**'s 'Nothing More' from *The Stones of Chile* translated by Dennis Maloney (White Pine Press, 1986) translation © Dennis Maloney (1986), poem © Pablo Neruda (1986); *Index on Censorship* for **Nguyen Chi Thien**'s 'I Kept Silent'.

◆ O ◆   Penguin Books for **Niyi Osundare**'s 'I Sing of Change' from *The Penguin Book of Modern African Poetry* edited by Gerald Moore and Ulli Beier (Third Edition, 1984) © Gerald Moore and Ulli Beier (1963, 1968, 1984).

◆ P ◆   Latin American Literary Review Press for **Renata Pallottini**'s 'The Shriek' from *Woman Who Has Sprouted Wings* edited by Mary Crow (1984) English translation © Latin American Literary Review Press; **Gieve Patel** for 'On Killing a Tree' © Gieve Patel; George Gömöri and Clive Wilmer for **György Petri**'s 'Night song of the personal shadow' and 'To be said over and over again' from *Night Song of the Personal Shadow: Selected Poems* translated by Clive Wilmer and George Gömöri (Bloodaxe Books, 1991) translation © Clive Wilmer and George Gömöri, poems György Petri; Sigurdur A. Magnússon for **Hannes Pétursson**'s 'The Crematorium in Dachau' © Sigurdur A. Magnússon; Anvil Press Poetry for **János Pilinszky**'s 'Apocrypha', 'Fable', 'The Passion' from *János Pilinszky: The Desert of Love* selected and translated by János Csokits and Ted Hughes (Anvil Press Poetry, 1989) © Péter Kovács (1989) translation © János Csokits and Ted Hughes (1976, 1989).

◆ Q ◆   Curbstone Press for **Jaime Suárez Quemain**'s 'And you again, Good Sir' from *On the Front Line: Guerrilla Poems of El Salvador* edited and translated by Claribel Alegría and Darwin J. Flakoll (Curbstone Press, 1989) translation Claribel Alegría and Darwin J. Flakoll (1989).

◆ R ◆   **Cecil Rajendra** for 'The Animal and Insect Act' from *Refugees and Other Despairs* (Choice Books, 1980); Northwestern University Press for **Irina Ratushinskaya**'s 'Give me a nickname, prison', 'We will not go into that river', 'Wildstrawberry Town' from *Beyond the Limit: Poems by Irina Ratushinskaya* translated by Frances Padorr Brent and Carol J. Avins (1987) translation © Frances Padorr Brent and Carol J. Avins (1987), Russian text © Irina Ratushinskaya (1987); David Ray for 'Propaganda' © David Ray (1991); Efstathiadis Group for Yannis Ritsos' 'Search' from *Yannis Ritsos: Selected Poems* translated by Nikos Stangos (1971, 1974, 1981) © Yannis Ritsos (1974, 1981); *Index on Censorship* for Mykola Rudenko's 'It's so easy: just recant'.

◆ S ◆   Curbstone Press for **Roberto Saballos**' 'A Story' from *On the Front Line: Guerrilla Poems of El Salvador* edited and translated by Claribel Alegría and Darwin J. Flakoll (Curbstone Press, 1989) translation Claribel Alegría and Darwin J. Flakoll (1989); **Olga Sedakova** for 'A Chinese journey' (extract) © Olga Sedakova; **Sipho Sepamla** for 'Talk to the Peach Tree' and 'Tell Me News'; **Mongane Wally Serote** for 'Ofay-Watcher Looks Back' from *Yakhal'inkomo* (Ad. Donker, 1972) © Mongane Wally Serote (1972); University of Hawaii Press for **Shao Yanxiang**'s 'I'll Always Remember' and 'My Optimism' from *The Red Azalea. Chinese Poetry since the Cultural Revolution* edited by Edward Morin and translated by Fang Dai, Dennis Ding and Edward Morin (1990) © University of Hawaii Press (1990); **Peggy Shumaker** for 'Blue Corn, Black Mesa' from *Esperanza's Hair* (University of Alabama Press, 1985) © Peggy Shumaker (1985); **R.A. Simpson** for 'Making a Myth' from *R.A. Simpson: Selected Poems* (University of Queensland Press, 1981) © University of Queensland Press (1981); James MacGibbon for **Stevie Smith**'s 'The Death Sentence' from *The Collected Poems of Stevie Smith* (Penguin Twentieth Century Classics); Forest Books for **Marin Sorescu**'s 'Competition' from *An Anthology of Contemporary Romanian Poetry* translated by Andrea Deletant and Brenda Walker (1984) translations © Andrea Deletant and Brenda Walker; Andre Deutsch, and Random House, Inc for **Wole Soyinka**'s 'After the Deluge' and 'The Apotheosis of Master Sergeant Doe' from *Mandela's Earth* (Methuen, 1990) © Wole Soyinka (1988); Faber & Faber for **Wallace Stevens**' 'The Man with the Blue Guitar' (extract) from *The Collected Poems of Wallace Stevens* (Alfred A. Knopf, 1965) © Wallace Stevens; Oxford University Press for **Anne Stevenson**'s 'Making Poetry' from *Selected Poems 1956-1986* © Anne Stevenson (1987);

Michael March for **Jana Štroblová**'s 'The Slaughterhouse' from *Child of Europe* edited by Michael March (Penguin Books, 1990) © Michael March (1990).

◆ **T** ◆ University of Pittsburgh Press for **Tomas Tranströmer**'s 'Open and Closed Rooms' from *Windows and Stones* translated by May Swenson with Leif Sjöberg (1972) © University of Pittsburgh Press (1972); Penguin Books for **Tsuboi Shigeji**'s 'Autumn in Gaol', 'English – Ugh!', 'Silent, but ...' from *The Penguin Book of Japanese Verse* translated by Geoffrey Bownas and Anthony Thwaite (1964) © Geoffrey Bownas and Anthony Thwaite (1964).

◆ **U** ◆ Kevin Hart for **Giuseppe Ungaretti**'s 'Fine Night' from *The Buried Harbour* translated by Kevin Hart (The Leros Press, 1990) © The Leros Press (1990).

◆ **W** ◆ **Chris Wallace-Crabbe** for 'A Wintry Manifesto' from *Selected Poems* (Angus & Robertson, 1973) © Chris Wallace-Crabbe, and 'Beijing', reprinted from the *Age*, **Archie Weller** for 'Willy-willy man' from *Inside Black Australia. An Anthology of Aboriginal Poetry* edited by Kevin Gilbert (Penguin Books Australia, 1988) collection © Kevin Gilbert (1988), poem © Archie Weller; Collins Angus & Robertson for **Judith Wright**'s 'Weapon' from *Judith Wright Collected Poems 1942-1970* (1971) © Judith Wright (1971).

◆ **Y** ◆ University of Hawaii Press for **Yang Lian**'s 'Plowing' from *The Red Azalea. Chinese Poetry since the Cultural Revolution* edited by Edward Morin and translated by Fang Dai, Dennis Ding and Edward Morin (1990) © University of Hawaii Press (1990); **Saul Yurkievich** for 'Sentence' translated by Cola Franzen; Penguin Books for **Sa'di Yusuf**'s 'Hamra Night' from *Modern Poetry of the Arab World* translated and edited by Abdullah al-Udhari (1986) © Abdullah al-Udhari (1986).

The editors and publishers have tried, without success, to trace and contact the poets or copyright-holders for the following poems. They would welcome any up-to-date information that would enable them to confirm permission:
Marcos Ana: 'A Short Letter to the World'; **Ernesto Cardenal**: 'Somoza Unveils the Statue of Somoza in Somoza Stadium'; **Edilberto Coutinho**: 'The fight goes on'; **Gloria Diéz**: 'Woman of Air, Woman of Water'; **Mbella Sonne Dipoko**: 'Pain'; **Mohan Koirala**: 'My Nepali words, broken, fragmented'; **Ana Iris Varas**: 'Untitled'.

Biographical notes and index

The page numbers in brackets at the end of each entry are the index to the poems by that writer. (N.B. In some Asian cultures the surname is given first but is still listed here in its alphabetical order.)

These biographical notes have been compiled from information supplied. If there are any inaccuracies, the editors would be grateful to be informed for correction in any future editions.

Jonathan Aaron (1941 -) was born in Massachusetts, USA, and studied at the universities of Chicago and Yale. He has had poems published in the *New York Review of Books, Paris Review,* and *Partisan Review.* His first book of poems, *Second Sight* (Harper & Row) was a winner of the 1982 National Poetry Series open competition, and his book, *Corridor,* will be published in 1992 by Wesleyan University Press. He teaches writing and rhetoric at Emerson College in Boston.   [35]

Robert Adamson (1943 -) was born in Sydney, Australia, and is a writer, editor and publisher. He is best known for his poetry which has been published widely and translated into seven languages. In collaboration with Bruce Hanford he wrote the novel, *Zimmer's Essay* (1974), and his own publications include *Swamp Riddles, Cross The Border, Where I Come From, The Law At Heart's Desire* and *Selected Poems.* He was instrumental in founding *New Poetry* magazine and directs Paper Bark Press. His book *The Clean Dark* (1990) won three of Australia's major poetry awards, and his autobiographical novella *Wards of the State* is due for publication in 1992.   [52]

Allen Afterman (1941 -) was born in Los Angeles and is a graduate of UCLA Harvard Law School and Monash University. In 1966 he left the USA and lived in New Zealand and Singapore. Since 1973 he has lived and worked on a farm in southern New South Wales, Australia.   [151]

Marjorie Agosin (1954 -) is a Chilean poet and writer living in the USA where she is a professor at Wellesley College. Her books of poetry include *Zones of Pain, Circles of Madness,* and *Sargasso.* She is the Latin American editor at White Pine Press and has recently edited two collections: *Landscapes of a New Land: Fiction by Latin American Women* and *Secret Weavers: Stories of the Fantastic.* [95, 124, 145]

Anna Akhmatova (1889 - 1966) was born in Odessa, and is considered by many to be one of the USSR's finest poets. In 1910 she married the poet Nikolai Gumilev. Together with Mandelstam (see below), they became the leaders of the new poetic movement, 'Acmeism'. Gumilev was shot by the Bolsheviks in 1921 as an alleged counter-revolutionary and, despite the fact that they had divorced three years earlier, she continued to suffer the political taint of their association. Practically none of her poetry was published between 1923 and 1940. Her son was arrested and sent to a labour camp, as was her lover, Nikolai Punin. After Stalin's death her poetry began to be published again, and she received an honorary D.Litt. from Oxford in 1965.   [30, 43, 53, 139]

Claribel Alegría (1924 -   ) was born in Nicaragua, but considers herself a Salvadoran, having grown up in that country. She attended George Washington University and travelled widely, living in Mexico, Chile, Uruguay and Europe. She lives in Nicaragua. She has written poetry, novels, short stories and children's stories, and in 1978 her book of poems, *Sobrevivo*, won Cuba's Casa de las Americas prize. She has also edited several anthologies and is a widely published translator.   [56]

Muhammad Àl-Maghut (1932 -   ) was born in Salamiya, Syria, and lives in Damascus. Self-educated, he works as a journalist and writes for television and the cinema. He has written three volumes of poetry and two plays.   [13]

Yehuda Amichai (1924 -   ) was born in Germany, brought up in an Orthodox Jewish environment and received a formal religious education. He moved to Palestine with his family in 1936, and much of his life has been lived in a land struggling to establish its identity. For many years he earned his living as a teacher. His first collection of poetry appeared in 1955. Since then he has published ten more volumes of poetry, as well as novels, short stories and plays. His poetry has been translated into some twenty languages.   [12]

Marcos Ana was a political prisoner in Burgos Jail for twenty-two years. His poem, 'A Short Letter to the World', is taken from *From Burgos Jail*.   [88]

W.H. Auden (1907 - 73) was raised in Birmingham, England, and studied at Oxford. After living for a time in Berlin, he returned to England to work as a teacher. His first volume of poetry, *Poems* (1930) established him as one of the most talented voices of his generation, and he continued to publish poetry, plays, libretti and other literary works. He became a US citizen in 1946, was elected professor of poetry at Oxford in 1956 and a fellow of Christ Church in 1962. He is widely regarded as one of the major poetic voices of the century.   [34]

James Baxter (1926 - 72) was born in Brighton, New Zealand, and studied at Otago, Canterbury and Victoria universities. He worked as a labourer, postman, editor and school teacher, and in 1969 founded a commune on the Wanganui River. As well as eighteen volumes of poetry, he wrote criticism, drama, prose and reviews. He received the MacMillan Brown poetry award, the Hubert Church memorial award, a Unesco fellowship in India in 1958, and was Robert Burns fellow at Otago University in 1966 and 1967.   [110]

Metija Bećković (1939 -   ) was born in Senta, and studied Yugoslav literature at the University of Belgrade. Since 1961 he has published several books of verse, and one of these, *Che* (1969), has been translated into English. He works as a writer in Belgrade. He is one of the finest poets in what used to be Yugoslavia.   [82]

Sherko Bekas (1940 -   ) was born in Sulaymaniya, southern Kurdistan (Iraq), the son of Faiq Berkas, one of the most famous Kurdish poets. He was educated in Sulaymaniya and Baghdad, and published his first collection of poems in 1968. His close association with the Kurdish Liberation Movement led to his exile for three years to southern Iraq in 1975. Since 1987 he has lived in Sweden. He has published seven volumes of collected verse, as well as two poetic stories and two plays in verse. In 1987 he was awarded the Swedish Pen Club's Tucholsky prize and the Freedom of the City of Florence. [159]

Horst Bienek (1930 - 91) was born in upper Silesia, Germany, and began his literary career as a journalist in Berlin, while studying with Brecht at the Berliner Ensemble. In 1951 he was arrested in East Berlin on a political charge and sentenced to twenty-five years forced labour, of which he served four in the prison camp of Vorkuta, in Russia. He was the recipient of a number of distinguished literary prizes. [50, 57]

Elizabeth Bishop (1911 - 79) was born in Worcester, Massachusetts, graduated from Vassar, and then travelled extensively, living in New York, Florida, and for seventeen years in Brazil. She taught at Harvard for seven years, at New York University, and at the Massachusetts Institute of Technology. Her first book of poetry, *North and South* (1946) won the Houghton Mifflin poetry award. For her second volume, *North and South and A Cold Spring* (1955) she received the Pulitzer prize. Her *Completed Poems* (1969) won the National Book award. In 1979 she became the first woman and the first American to win the prestigious Books award/Neustadt international prize for literature. [40]

Rosalind Brackenbury (1942 -) was born in London and educated at Sherborne School for Girls and Girton College, Cambridge. She has published eight novels and two collections of poetry. She writes regularly for the magazine, *Resurgence*, and has contributed to two books on writing. In 1988 - 89 she had a Scottish Arts Council travel grant to go to Australia, and in 1990 - 91, she was writer-in-residence in Dumfries and Galloway, Scotland. [25]

R.F. Brissenden (1928 - 91) was born in New South Wales, Australia, and studied at Sydney and Leeds universities. From 1953 he pursued an academic career, and retired from the Australian National University in 1985 as reader in English. He was the first literary editor of the *Australian* newspaper and later chairman of the literature board of the Australia Council. Well-known as a poet and critic, he also wrote first-class thrillers. In 1982 he was awarded the Order of Australia. [140]

Dennis Brutus (1924 -) was born in Zimbabwe but grew up in South Africa. He taught English and Afrikaans in high school for fourteen years until he was dismissed in 1962 for his anti-apartheid activities. While studying law at the University of Witwatersrand, Johannesburg, he became increasingly active in the struggle against racism in South African sports. He was arrested, banned, shot in an attempt to leave South Africa and sentenced to eighteen month's hard labour. After his release he was banned and went to London in 1966. He is now teaching at the University of Pittsburgh. He is one of South Africa's best known and most highly regarded poets. [118, 125, 153]

Vincent Buckley (1925 - 88) was born in Victoria, Australia, and educated at the universities of Melbourne and Cambridge. He served in the RAAF during World War II, and for many years was professor of English at the University of Melbourne. He was poetry editor of the *Bulletin* magazine 1961-63 and published several volumes of poetry and essays. His autobiography *Cutting Green Hay* was published in 1983, and *Memory Ireland* in 1985. His *Last Poems* appeared in 1991, together with his anthology, the *Faber Book of Modern Australian Verse*. [81, 112, 117]

Ion Caraion is generally recognised as one of the major voices in post-war Romanian poetry. He has written fifteen books of poetry, many critical essays, and has translated and edited a number of other works. He was imprisoned for eleven years during the Stalin era, and his poetry was banned between 1948 and 1965. He lives in Bucharest. [107]

Ernesto Cardenal (1925 -) was born in Granada, and studied literature and philosophy at the University of Mexico. In 1950, after graduate studies at Columbia University, he returned to Nicaragua and became involved in revolutionary activities. In 1957 he entered the Trappist monastery in Kentucky and became a disciple of Thomas Merton. He was ordained a Roman Catholic priest in 1965 and set up a contemplative commune in Nicaragua the following year. This commune was destroyed by Somoza's National Guard in 1977. Following the Sandinista victory in 1979 he was appointed minister of culture. He is widely regarded as one of Latin America's leading poets. [32, 105]

Nina Cassian (1924 -) was born in Galati, Romania, and studied painting and drama in Bucharest. Her first volume of verse, *La Scara 1/1* appeared in 1948. In addition to poetry, she has composed chamber and symphonic music and illustrated some of her own books. Since 1985 she has been living in New York. A selection of her poems, *Lady of Miracles*, was published in 1982. [62]

Ross Clark (1953 -) was born in Toowoomba, Australia, and completed his tertiary studies in English at the University of Queensland. He has published two volumes of poetry, edited and contributed to another, and co-edited a book of children's writing. He has also written short stories and reviews, and is involved internationally with the writing, editing and judging of haiku. He is a secondary-school teacher in Brisbane. [142]

David Constantine (1944 -) was born in Lancashire, England, and is a fellow in German at Queen's College, Oxford. Bloodaxe Books published his two collections of poetry, *A Brightness to Cast Shadows* (1980) and *Watching for Dolphins* (1983). In 1984 he won the Alice Hunt Bartlett award, and his critical introduction to the poetry of Hölderlin was published by Oxford University Press in 1985. [132]

Edilberto Coutinho (1938 -) holds a degree in law but works as a journalist and author. His favourite genre is the short story, although he also writes essays, critical anthologies, biographical studies and poetry. He began working as a journalist for *Jornal do Brasil*, the leading newspaper in Rio de Janeiro, and for three years was a correspondent in Europe. Two of his best-known works are *Um Negro vai à Forra* (A Black Man Gets Even), and *Presença Poética do Recife* (Poetic Presence of Recife). [134]

Alison Croggon (1962 -) was born in Carltonville, South Africa, went to Australia at the age of seven, attended school in Ballarat, and completed a cadetship in journalism. Since 1985 she has worked as a freelance journalist, is Melbourne theatre critic for the *Bulletin* magazine and poetry editor of

Modern Writing. Her poems have appeared in magazines in Australia and overseas, and in various anthologies. She was awarded the Victorian Council for the Arts poetry fellowship in 1989. Her first collection of poems, *This is the Stone*, was published by Penguin Books in 1991. [36]

Mahmoud Darwish (1942 -) was born in the village of al-Barweh, Palestine. He worked as a journalist in Haifa until he left Israel in 1972 for Beirut, where he remained until 1982. He lives in Paris and edits the magazine *Al-Karmal*. He was awarded the Lotus prize in 1969 and the Lenin prize in 1983. [23]

Bruce Dawe (1930 -) was born in Geelong, Australia, and attended Northcote High School in Melbourne. After leaving school he worked at many jobs, including farm-hand, copy-boy, postman and gardener, before joining the Royal Australian Air Force in 1959. In 1968 he began a teaching career at Downlands College, Toowoomba. He has published ten books of poetry, one book of short stories, one book of essays, and has edited two other books. He has received numerous awards for his poetry, including: The Ampol Arts award for creative literature (1967), the Grace Levin poetry prize (1978), the Braille book of the year (1979), the Patrick White literary award (1980), the Christopher Brennan award (1984). He is widely recognised as Australia's most popular poet. [158]

Gloria Diéz (1949 -) was born in Langreo, Spain. She works as a television critic for *Diario 16*. [130]

Mircea Dinescu (1950 -) was born in Slobozia, Romania. His first poem was published in 1967. For many years he worked for the newspaper *România Literară* but was placed under house arrest in 1989 for speaking out against the Ceaucescu regime and the way it affected writers. With Ceaucescu's downfall he was carried on a tank to the TV station where he was one of the first to tell the Romanian people they were free. Since then he has been President of the Bucharest Writer's Union. His poetry has been translated into many languages. He is married and has two children. [75]

Mbella Sonne Dipoko (1936 -) was born at Mungo, Cameroon, and educated in that country and Nigeria. He moved to Paris in 1960, devoting himself mainly to writing and painting. He has published two novels, *A Few Nights and Days* (1966), and *Because of Women* (1974). [109]

Doan Van Minh (1950 -) was born in a village in North Vietnam. His father was beaten to death because he had been a village chairman under French occupation. Doan Van Minh started writing poetry when he was eighteen, and it was when discussing poetry with friends that he was interrupted by the police, who found his poems. He endured over twenty years of imprisonment, alternating with surveillance. He reached Hong Kong by boat in 1989 to become one of 8,000 inmates in the Whitehead refugee camp. [46]

Ariel Dorfman (1942 -) was a professor of journalism and literature in Chile during the Allende period. Since the 1973 coup he has lived in exile in the USA. As well as poetry he has written novels and essays and co-authored the popular *How To Read Donald Duck*, which has appeared in thirteen languages. [96]

Duoduo (1951 -   ) was born in Beijing and started writing poetry during the Cultural Revolution (1966 - 76). Before leaving China for Britain he worked as a journalist with a national newspaper, and in 1989 was awarded the *Today* prize for his collection, *Licheng*. Duoduo arrived in Britain for a prearranged poetry-reading tour on 5 June 1989, having been present at Tiananmen on the night, and day, of the massacre.   [26]

Faiz Ahmad Faiz (1911 - 84) was born in Sialkot, Punjab, and had a varied career as teacher, army officer, journalist, political leader, trade unionist and broadcaster. Imprisoned more than once by the Pakistani government for his political stance, he spent a period of exile with the Palestinians in Beirut. He returned to Pakistan in 1984, where he died in Lahore. Faiz received many literary awards, notably the Lenin prize.   [161]

Ahmad Faraz (1936 -   ) was born in Kohat, Pakistan. He is a leading Urdu poet, and in recent years his poetry has taken on distinctively socialist and progressive themes. He was jailed in Pakistan for his outspoken rejection of military rule, and lived in exile in Britain. After Zia's demise, Faraz returned to Pakistan to become the director-general of the Academy of Letters. He lives in Islamabad.   [51, 86]

Elaine Feinstein (1930 -   ) was born in Lancashire, England, and educated at Wyggeston Grammar School and Newnham College, Cambridge. She worked for a number of years as a lecturer in English and, as well as poetry, has written novels and short stories. She has also translated *The Selected Poems of Marina Tsvetayeva* (OUP, 1971).   [138]

Basil Fernando, of Sinhalese origin, began writing poetry at high school. He studied law, and for years after graduation worked as a teacher of English in Colombo. In 1984 he started to work as a human-rights lawyer, covering cases that involved torture or extra-judicial killing by the security forces. Four of his colleagues were killed within six months and he was told that his safety could not be guaranteed. He works in Hong Kong as an appeal lawyer for the United Nations high commissioner for refugees.   [47]

Janet Frame (1924 -   ) was born in Dunedin, New Zealand, and educated at Otago University. From 1956 - 61 she lived in London. Apart from her highly acclaimed three-volume autobiography, she has written eleven novels. She has been awarded the New Zealand literary award for non-fiction, the James Wattie book of the year award (1983 and 1985) and the Commonwealth Literary award for her novel *The Carpathians* in 1989.   [154]

Gao Falin (1950 -   ) is a graduate of Wuhan University and a member of the Chinese Writers' Association. He has published three collections of poetry and has been awarded the National prize for poetry.   [14]

Gary Geddes (1940 -   ) was born in Vancouver, British Columbia, and studied at the universities of British Columbia, Reading and Toronto, receiving a PhD in English. He has been active as a poet, fiction writer, playwright, editor, anthologist, critic and publisher, and his works have won numerous prizes and awards. He teaches at Concordia University in Montreal. His recent publications are *No Easy Exit/Salida Dificil, Light of Burning Towers: Poems New and Selected*, and *Letters from Managua: Meditations on Politics and Art.* [94]

Mary Gilmore (1865 - 1962) was born in Australia, in rural New South Wales, and spent her early years travelling with her father in the outback. She became a teacher, was strongly involved in the women's movement in the 1890s and became the first female member of the Australian Workers Union. She was also part of a utopian socialist settlement in Paraguay. After returning to Australia in 1902, she wrote for the *Bulletin* and the *Worker*, and wrote books of poetry and prose, continuing her strong socialist critique of Australian society. At 72 she was made a Dame of the British Empire. [145]

Robert Gray (1945 -) grew up in Coffs Harbour, Australia, left school early and has worked as an advertising copywriter, bookshop assistant and freelance journalist. He has received numerous fellowships from the Australia Council. His *Piano* was published in 1988, and his *Selected Poems* in 1985 (revised 1990). [55]

Ferreira Gullar (1930 -) was born in Brazil, in São Luís do Maranhão, and moved to Rio in 1951. He was in the forefront of the Brazilian avant-garde until 1962, and then focussed more seriously on social problems. An opponent of the military regime established in 1964, he lived in exile from 1971 - 77. He works as an art critic and television writer. [24]

Thom Gunn (1929 -) was born in England, and studied at University College School in London and at Cambridge University. In 1954 he went to Stanford University as a student and teacher. He was a leading figure in 'The Movement' in England in the 1950s, but has lived for many years in the USA. He currently teaches at the University of California (Berkeley). [113]

Kevin Hart (1954 -) was born in London and studied English at the Australian National University and the University of Melbourne. He has published four volumes of poetry, a major work of criticism, *The Trespass of the Sign: Deconstruction, Theology and Philosophy* (Cambridge University Press, 1989), and a work of translation, *The Buried Harbour: Selected Poems of Giuseppe Ungaretti* (Leros Press, 1990). He is a member of the department of English at Monash University. [61]

Gwen Harwood (1920 -) was born in Brisbane, Australia, and educated at Brisbane Girls' Grammar School. She has published poetry, short stories, reviews and written libretti for a number of composers. She was awarded an honorary doctorate of letters by the University of Tasmania in 1988, and has also received a number of literary awards, including the Robert Frost award in 1977, the Patrick White award in 1978, and the National poetry award in 1990. In 1992 she was federal president of the Fellowship of Australian Writers. She lives in Hobart, Tasmania. [126, 160]

Seamus Heaney (1939 -) was born in County Derry, Northern Ireland, and educated at Queens University, Belfast. He left Northern Ireland in 1972 and now lives in Dublin. He is widely recognised as one of the world's major English-speaking poets. As well as many volumes of poetry he has written critical essays, and, together with Ted Hughes (see below), edited the anthology, *The Rattle Bag*. He spends part of each year in the USA, where he teaches at Harvard University. In 1990 he was elected to the Chair of Poetry at Oxford University. [170]

Zbigniew Herbert (1924 -) was born in Poland, took part in the resistance movement, and after the war studied at Cracow and Warsaw universities. He has been translated into almost every European language, and has been awarded numerous prizes, among them the Jurzykowski prize (1964), the Austrian Government prize for European literature (1965) and the Petrarch prize (1979). His *Selected Poems* was published in English in 1968. [37]

Miroslav Holub (1923 -) is a distinguished Czechoslovakian research chemist and one of his country's leading poets. The first English translation of his work, *Selected Poems*, appeared in 1967. *On the Contrary and Other Poems* (1982) represents a decade of his work. [90]

A.D. Hope (1907 -) was born in Cooma, Australia, and spent his childhood in country Tasmania, where his father served as a Presbyterian minister. He was educated at Sydney and Oxford universities. Before his appointment as professor of English at the Australian National University, he worked as a teacher, psychologist and lecturer. He has published six books of poetry as well as literary essays and criticism. He received the Robert Frost award for poetry in 1976, and has been awarded honorary doctorates at both Monash and Melbourne universities. [136]

Ted Hughes (1930 -) was born in Yorkshire, England, attended a local grammar school, and completed two years' national aervice before going to Cambridge. He began studying English, but changed to a course in archaeology and anthropology. As well as poetry, he has written short stories, libretti and critical essays. He has also been a strong advocate of other poets, including the Hungarian, János Pilinszky (see below). He was a founder of *Modern Poetry in Translation*, a magazine that set the pattern for poetry translation in the 1960s. [150]

Habib Jalib (1929 -) was born in Pakistan and is one of that country's most popular poets, particularly among students. [164]

Evan Jones (1931 -) was born in Melbourne, Australia, and took degrees in history and English at the universities of Melbourne and Stanford. He has published four volumes of verse and co-edited *Poems of Kenneth Mackenzie* (Angus & Robertson). [163, 166]

Mohan Koirala (1926 -) was born in Kathmandu, Nepal. He worked for many years as a teacher and has published seven books of poetry. He was a member of the Royal Nepal Academy from 1974 - 79, and was re-admitted again in 1990. He is also a member of the banned Nepal Congress Party. [27]

Grandfather Koori was born "in the Beginning" in the heart of the red, sandy Mallee country in Wiradjuriland, somewhere near Ivanhoe. Tribe, Wiradjuri-Nghulli: *Murar ar ao Radthuri. Red Kangaroo Man.* [44]

Iva Kotrla (1947 -), a poet and mother of six children, was harassed and called to interrogation by the Czechoslovakian government for the offence of writing poetry, only a few weeks after the birth of her fifth child. While still in hospital her home was searched and all her writing since 1966 was confiscated. [144]

Ivan Kraus (1939 -) was born in Prague, studied at the School of International Economic Relations, and was one of the artists who started the first Black Theatre of Prague in the 1960s. He left Czechoslovakia in 1968 after the Russian occupation and has since lived in Paris and Baden-Baden. He has published five books, receiving awards for his work in Czechoslovakia, USA, and Germany. His poem, 'The Censor' was first performed in a program 'Dancing Two-gether' at a theatre festival in Vermont, USA, in 1984. [69]

Maxine Kumin (1925 -) was born in Philadelphia, USA, and was educated at Radcliffe College. She taught English at various universities including Princeton and Columbia. She has received many prizes and awards, including the Pulitzer prize (1973) and the American Academy award (1980). As well as poetry, she has written novels, short stories, children's literature and essays. [146]

Kim Kwang-sŏp (1905 - 77) was born in north-east Korea and, after graduating from high school, studied English literature in Tokyo. After returning to Seoul, he worked as a high-school teacher and in 1941 was imprisoned for preaching anti-Japanese sentiments. After the liberation he was active as a champion of anti-Leftist literary movements. He held a number of high offices, and was awarded many honours, including the Korean Academy of Art prize in 1974. [120]

Christine Lavant (1915 - 73) was born in the Lavant Valley in Austria, the ninth child of a miner. Ill throughout her life and later deaf and blind, she earned her living by knitting. As well as her poetry she published five volumes of stories and a radio play. [143]

D.H. Lawrence (1885 - 1930) was born in the English Midlands, the son of a miner. He trained as a teacher but then travelled widely, writing a series of highly original short stories, novels and poems. He was also a gifted painter. His novels in particular hold a central place in modern English literature. [76]

Liang Xiaobin (1955 -) was born in Shandong province, China. During the Cultural Revolution he worked as a peasant in the countryside. He has also been a factory worker. He began to publish his poetry in 1979. [66]

James McAuley (1917 - 76) was born in Sydney, Australia, and educated at Sydney University. He became well known as a poet and critic through his contributions to periodicals, the 'Ern Malley' literary hoax, and his volumes of poetry. In 1952 he converted to Catholicism. His career spanned war work in the Australian Army Directorate of Research and Civil Affairs, lecturer in government at the Australian School of Pacific Administration, editor of the literary magazine, *Quadrant*, in 1956, and professor of English at the University of Tasmania in 1961. [74]

Circe Maia (1932 -) was born in Montevideo, Uruguay, and now lives in Tacuarembo, where she teaches philosophy at high-school level. Her first book of poetry was published when she was eleven, and by 1992 she had published five others. [168]

Desanka Maksimović (1898 -   ) was born in Rabrovica, Yugoslavia, and studied in Belgrade and Paris. She taught for many years and, after World War I, began to write poetry and literature for children. After World War II her poetry began to express increasing concern for the suffering of her people.   [98]

Osip Mandelstam (1891 - 1938) was brought up in St Petersburg and studied at the universities of Heidelberg and St Petersburg, as well as in France and Italy. Together with Akhmatova (see above), he was a member of the poetic movement, 'Acmeism', and was persecuted by the Soviet authorities. He was arrested and exiled in 1934 for having written the poem included in this anthology, 'The Stalin Epigram'. Under intense psychological and physical torment, his condition deteriorated rapidly, and, rearrested in 1938, he died on his way to a Siberian labour camp.   [12, 20, 102, 137]

W.S. Merwin (1927 -   ) grew up in the USA, in New Jersey and Pennsylvania, and in his early twenties worked as a tutor in Europe. He then made the greater part of his living as a translator. In addition to poetry, he has written prose, articles and radio scripts. He was awarded the Pulitzer prize for *The Carrier of Ladders* (1970) and the PEN Translation prize for *Selected Translations (1948 - 1968)* (1968). In 1974 he was awarded the fellowship of the Academy of American Poets, and in 1979 he was awarded the Bollingen prize for poetry. [92]

Czeslaw Milosz (1911 -   ) was born in Lithuania. He was one of the leaders of the avant-garde poetry movement in Poland in the 1930s, was in the resistance during World War II, and edited an anti-Nazi anthology. After several years in the diplomatic service he severed his ties with the post-war Polish government and emigrated to the USA. He teaches at the University of California (Berkeley). As well as poetry he has written novels and criticism and received the Neustadt international prize for literature in 1978. His *Selected Poems* was published in English in 1973.   [93]

Miguel Huezo Mixco was, in 1991, a combatant in the El Salvadoran *Frente Farabundo Martí de Liberacion Nacional.*   [17]

R. H. Morrison (1915 -   ) was born in Melbourne, Australia, and studied Russian at the University of Melbourne. He is the author of twenty books of poetry and verse translation, a prose memoir on V.G. Szobovits and a number of essays, and edited *Vietnam Voices*, an anthology published as a special issue of *Overland* magazine (1973). He was a prize-winner in the 1990 International Haiku Contest, Japan. He devotes time every month to Amnesty letter-writing, considering this a writer's duty and a free person's privilege.   [115]

Es'kia Mphahlele (1919 -   ) was born in Pretoria, South Africa. He completed a PhD in creative writing at the University of Denver, and has taught at many universities in the USA and Africa. In 1992 he was emeritus professor of literature at the University of Witwatersrand. As well as poetry he has written short stories, novels, literary criticism, and two autobiographical works: *Down Second Avenue* and *Afrika My Music.*   [133]

Lupenga Mphande (1947 -   ) was born in northern Malawi, and studied English and history at the University of Malawi and applied linguistics at the

University of Lancaster. He also holds an honorary doctorate in literature. He is editor of *Odi*, a bilingual journal of literature published in Malawi, and has co-edited an anthology of short stories. He lectures at the University of Malawi. [106]

Mbuyiseni Oswald Mtshali (1940 -   ) was educated at the University of South Africa and at the New School for Social Research in New York, majoring in English and education. He has worked in a wide number of occupations, including journalism and teaching. He has published two books of poems. [104]

Les Murray (1938 -   ) was born in rural New South Wales, Australia, and educated at country schools and Sydney University. Among a number of jobs he has had was translator of western European languages at the Australian National University. As well as poetry, he has written criticism and essays, and has also edited two anthologies. In 1970 he won the New South Wales Captain Cook Bicentenary poetry prize. Some years ago, he returned to live again in the farming country of northern New South Wales.   [148]

Kishwar Naheed (1940 -   ) was born in Bulundshehr, India, and educated at Punjab University. She has worked as a journalist and translator, and director of Lahore Arts Council. She is considered a leading poet in Urdu, and has translated poets such as Pablo Neruda (see below) into that language. She lives in Pakistan.   [67]

Pablo Neruda (1904 - 73) was born in Parral, Chile, and studied in Santiago. He published his first two books of poems in 1921 and 1923, which won him instant recognition, and he went on to become one of Latin America's most acclaimed poets. He was Chilean consul in Rangoon, Java and Barcelona, was greatly influenced by events in the Spanish Civil War, and joined the Communist Party after World War II. He was awarded the Nobel prize for poetry in 1971, and from 1970 to 1973 was Chilean ambassador to Paris.   [164]

Nguyen Chi Thien was first detained in North Vietnam in 1958 for speaking against the authorities. He has spent twenty years of his life in prison camps. In 1979 he entered the British embassy in Hanoi seeking asylum but was refused. He handed over a collection of his poems and a letter imploring the world to publicise the conditions in the prison camps. On leaving the embassy he was immediately arrested and in 1992 was still in Hoa Lo Central prison in Hanoi.   [119]

Niyi Osundare (1947 -   ) was born in Ondo State, Nigeria, and studied at Ibadan, Leeds and Toronto. His collection, *The Eye of the Earth* (1986), was joint winner of the 1986 Commonwealth poetry prize. As well as poetry, he has written several plays. In 1992 he was a lecturer in English at the University of Ibadan, Nigeria.   [167]

Renata Pallottini (1937 -   ) was born in Sao Paolo, Brazil. She studied law and philosophy and practiced law for two years. She later turned to work in the theatre and in 1992 was teaching at the University Theatre in Sao Paolo. She has published many books of poems and written a number of plays, receiving awards for both.   [91]

Gieve Patel (1940 -) was born in Bombay and educated at St Xavier's High School and Grant Medical College. In 1992 he was living in Bombay where he is a general practitioner. As well as writing he also paints. He is one of India's leading poets and his work has been published in two volumes: *Poems* (1966) and *How Do You Withstand, Body* (1976). He has also written the following plays: *Princes* (1970), *Savaksa* (1982) and *Mister Behram* (1987). [64]

György Petri (1943 -) was born in Budapest, Hungary, and studied philosphy and psychology at the University of Budapest. He is one of the leading voices in contemporary Hungarian poetry. In 1989 two collections, *It Exists Somewhere* and *Whatever was Left Out*, sold out on publication. His *Collected Poems* and an English selection, *Night Song of the Personal Shadow* (Bloodaxe Books), appeared in 1991. [82, 103]

Hannes Pétursson (1931 -) was born in Saudárkrókur, north Iceland, completed studies in Germanistics in Cologne and Heidelberg, and graduated from the University of Iceland in Icelandic philology. For many years he worked for the Cultural Fund of Iceland, and since 1976 has devoted himself to writing. As well as editing and translating a number of books, he has written poetry, short stories, biographies, thrillers and criticism. He has been awarded a number of Icelandic literary prizes. [31]

János Pilinszky (1921 - 81) was born in Budapest, Hungary. After being conscripted for military service in 1944, he was captured and spent two years in German prison camps. His first collection of poems appeared in 1946. Although his poetic output has been relatively small, he is widely regarded as one of Hungary's most distinctive poets. [58, 123, 128]

Jaime Suárez Quemain (1950 - 80) was the editor of an independent newspaper when he was arrested by plainclothes men in a San Salvador cafe in 1980. His mutilated body was discovered the following day. [22]

Cecil Rajendra (1941 -) was born in Penang, Malaysia, and educated at St Xavier's Institution, the University of Singapore and Lincoln's Inn, London. He was chairman of the Malaysian Bar Council's legal aid scheme from 1986 - 90, and in 1992 was chairman of both the Legal Aid Centre, which he founded, and of the Penang Bar Human Rights Group. Because of their 'sensitive' nature, his poems are published abroad. His poem 'The Animal and Insect Act' is his lawyer-poet's answer to laws in Malaysia that deal with freedom of expression and of assembly. He has published eleven volumes of poetry; his *Lovers, Lunatics & Lallang* was published by Bogle-L'ouverture Publications in 1989. [72]

Irina Ratushinskaya (1954 -) was born in Odessa, Ukraine, and studied physics at the University of Odessa. While lecturing at the Odessa Pedagogical Institute she began her serious commitment to writing poetry and to the human rights movement. The consequence of this was her sentence in 1983 to seven years of hard labour. After more than three years of hardship and deprivation, and as a result of sustained international protest, she was released. She now lives in the UK. [131, 152, 169]

David Ray (1932 -) was born in Oklahoma, USA, graduated from the

University of Chicago, and has taught at universities in the USA, India, New Zealand and Australia. He has written twelve books of poetry, several of which have won major awards. He also writes fiction and drama. In 1992 he was professor of English at the University of Missouri – Kansas City. [70]

Yannis Ritsos (1909 - 90) was born in Monemvasia, Greece. In 1926 he went to Athens where he worked briefly as a law clerk before becoming severely ill with tuberculosis and spending the next three years in sanatoriums. He subsequently worked in theatrical groups and became active in the left-wing revolutionary movement in Greece in the 1930s. His first book of poems, *Tractors*, was published in 1934, and it took him to the forefront of the new poetic movement in his country. Throughout his life he was repeatedly persecuted because of his political sympathies. He published over eighty-five collections and his poetry has appeared in translation in forty-five languages. [77]

Mykola Rudenko (1920 -   ) was born in Ukraine and fought with the Soviet army during World War II. Between 1946 and the late 1960s, he became a major literary figure in his country. He was editor of the Kiev literary journal, *DNIPRO*, and secretary of the Ukranian Union of Writers. He published over thirty books, including poetry, fiction and drama. In the 1970s he began to challenge Soviet policies. His writing was banned and he lost his livelihood. He joined the Moscow branch of Amnesty International in 1975, and in 1977 he was sentenced to seven years' imprisonment and five years' internal exile. In 1986 he was joined in exile by his wife, Raisa Rudenko, who had been serving a prison term for 'anti-Soviet agitation and propaganda'. Both were released from internal exile in 1987. [80]

Roberto Saballos was assassinated in El Salvador by a death squad in 1980. [85]

Olga Sedakova (1949 -   ) was born in Moscow and educated at Moscow State University and the Institute of Balkan and Slavonic Studies. She has published three volumes of poetry and has also written prose, essays, philological studies, criticism and translations. She has won a number of poetry prizes and her poems have been translated into a number of languages. She lectures in general poetics at Moscow University. [21]

Sipho Sepamla (1932 -   ) was born near Krugersdorp, South Africa, and in 1992 was director of the FUBA Academy in Johannesburg. He has been a teacher, impresario and editor, of both the magazine *New Classic*, which published much of the new South African black poetry, and *Sketch*, a black theatre review. He has published six volumes of his own poetry, including *From Gore to Soweto* in 1989, and four novels, including *A Scattered Survival*, also in 1989. He has travelled widely in Africa and Europe, has won several awards, including the French order of the arts and literature, and is involved in a number of community organisations. [19, 116]

Mongane Wally Serote (1944 -   ) was born in Johannesburg, and was educated there and at Columbia University. He was imprisoned for nine months under the Terrorism Act in 1969 - 70. He has written short stories and a novel, *To Every Birth Its Blood*. [18]

Shao Yanxiang (1933 -   ) was born in Beijing and left school at sixteen to work at the Radio Beijing broadcasting station. He wrote many poems in praise of the new China, but gradually began to write satirical essays that ridiculed the shortcomings of officials and bureaucrats. He was severely criticised and denounced as a rightist during the anti-rightist campaign of 1957 - 58. He is a former editor of China's leading poetry journal, *Poetry Magazine*, and has been a writer in residence at the University of Iowa.   [155, 156]

Peggy Shumaker (1952 -   ) was born in California and completed her formal education at the University of Arizona. As well as two volumes of poetry, she has published widely in journals, and has also written short prose and reviews. She has been awarded a National Endowment for the Arts fellowship in poetry. In 1992 she was associate professor and head of the English department at the University of Alaska, and lived in a log house outside Ester, Alaska.   [163]

R.A. Simpson (1929 -   ) was born in Melbourne, Australia, and educated at the Royal Melbourne Institute of Technology. His *Selected Poems* was published in 1981, and *Words For a Journey* in 1986. He taught 'Art and Literature' at the Chisholm Institute of Technology from 1968 until 1987 and, since 1969, has been poetry editor of the *Age* newspaper. A new collection of his poems and drawings was published in 1991.   [41]

Stevie Smith (1902 - 71) was born in Hull, England, and brought up in London where she spent most of her adult life working as a secretary. She wrote three novels and eight volumes of poetry, much of it illustrated by her own comic drawings. She was an accomplished reader of her own verse and found a new young audience at the readings that flourished in the 1960s. Her *Collected Poems* appeared in 1975.   [114]

Marin Sorescu (1936 -   ) was born in the Romanian village of Bulzeşti, the fifth child of a family of peasants. He studied philology at Iaşi University and since 1978 has been working as editor-in-chief of the literary review *Ramuri*. His first volume of poetry appeared in 1964, followed by many others, as well as by volumes of prose and drama. In 1974 he was awarded the prize for drama by the Writers' Union of Romania, and, in 1978, the international prize Le Muze by the Academia delle Muze, Florence. In 1983 he received the International Poetry prize 'Fernando Riello' in Madrid. His work has been translated into most languages.   [48]

Wole Soyinka (1934 -   ) was born in Nigeria, and educated there and at Leeds University. He worked in British theatre before returning to West Africa in 1960. He was for many years professor of comparative literature at Obafemi Awolowo University, Nigeria, and in 1986 became the first African writer to win the Nobel prize for literature. His writing includes plays, novels and poetry, and his volume of poems *A Shuttle in the Crypt* (1972) was written during a period of over two years in prison without trial.   [100, 108]

Wallace Stevens (1879 - 1955) was born in Pennsylvania, USA, and educated at Harvard University. He became a lawyer and worked in that profession throughout his life. His first volume of poetry, *Harmonium*, was published in 1923. This was followed by other collections, and his *Collected Poems* was published in 1954. He is one of the century's major American, and English-speaking, poets. [28]

Anne Stevenson (1933 -) was born in England of American parents, completed her education in the USA, and returned to England in 1954. She worked as a teacher in both countries, and held numerous posts in writing in the UK. For two years she was an arts fellow at Lady Margaret Hall, Oxford, in 1981 became Northern Arts literary fellow, and in 1992 was a member of the Arts Council literature panel. She has published nine volumes of poetry. [16]

Jana Štroblová (1936 -) was born in Prague, Czechoslovakia. She published four books of poetry before the Soviet and Warsaw Pact intervention of 1968. She was forced to leave her work as an editor of children's literature and was unable to publish for the next ten years. During the 1970s she did translation work under an assumed name. *Witchery* was published in 1989. [122]

Tomas Tranströmer (1931 -) is generally regarded as the leading voice in Swedish poetry, and divides his time between writing and working as a psychologist. His first book of verse was published when he was twenty-three and eight books have followed since. His *Selected Poems* was published in English in 1972, and *The Wild Market Square* in 1985. [165]

Tsuboi Shigeji (1889 - 1975) was a founder of the Japan Proletarian Writers League journal, *Red and Black*, and one of that movement's leading poets. As a member of the League, he was imprisoned twice for his leftist position. [65, 78, 123]

Giuseppe Ungaretti (1888 - 1970) was born in Alexandria, Egypt, of Italian parents and lived in Alexandria until he was twenty-four. He studied at the Sorbonne and later volunteered for service in World War I. For a number of years he was a journalist and correspondent, and in 1936, he moved to Sao Paolo, Brazil, to teach Italian language and literature. In 1942 he returned to Italy to take up the chair of modern and contemporary Italian literature at Rome University. His *Porto Sepolto* (1916) has been translated by Kevin Hart (see above) as *The Buried Harbour*. [162]

Ana Iris Varas was arrested by the Chilean authorities for distributing anti-government leaflets. She was imprisoned for seven months and released in December 1987. [84]

Chris Wallace-Crabbe (1934 -) holds a personal chair in Australian literature at the University of Melbourne; his criticism and poetry have been published extensively. He was Harkness fellow at Yale from 1965 - 67 and visiting fellow at Exeter in 1973. In 1988 he was visiting professor of Australian studies at Harvard University and in 1992 director of the Australian Studies Centre at the University of Melbourne. He has published twelve volumes of poetry and edited four anthologies. [38, 45]

Archie Weller (1957 -) was born in Subiaco, Western Australia, and grew up in the bush country south of Perth. In his early teenage years, his family moved to East Perth, a poor area full of "bikies, methos, migrants and Aboriginal families". He spent a year at the Western Australian Institute of Technology, and then began to write his first book, *The Day of the Dog*. His other books are

Going Home, and, co-edited with Colleen Francis-Glass, *Us Fellas*, an anthology of Aboriginal writings.   [11]

Judith Wright (1915 -   ) was born in Armidale, Australia, and grew up on farms in country New South Wales. Her formal schooling did not begin until she was thirteen and she completed her education at Sydney University. After travelling in Europe she returned to Australia and has become one of the country's pre-eminent literary figures, showing strong public concern for the injustices suffered by Australia's indigenous people. As well as her many volumes of poetry, she has written children's books, criticism, articles, essays and a social history, *The Generation of Men*.   [54]

Yang Lian (1955 -   ) was born in Berne, Switzerland, and returned to China with his parents in his first year. His poems have appeared in major national magazines, and he has worked for the Central Broadcasting station in Beijing. Several of his books were banned in 1987, yet he continued to write and published a major work of criticism, *The Self-Awareness of Man*. In 1989 he emigrated with his wife and child to New Zealand, and recently moved to Australia.   [15]

Saul Yurkievich (1931 -   ) was born in La Plata, Argentina. In the late 1960s he moved to Paris where he was appointed professor of Latin American literature at the Université de Paris VIII, a post he still occupied in 1992. He is a member of the editorial board of the international literary collective CHANGE, and served as president of the Instituto Internacional de Literatura Iberoamericana from 1981 - 83. He has published numerous books of poetry, criticism and translation.   [68]

Sa'di Yusuf (1934 -   ) was born in Basra, Iraq, and educated at the Bagdad Teachers' Training College. A former member of the Iraqi Communist Party, he was in Beirut during Israel's invasion of Lebanon in 1982. In 1992 he was living in Cyprus. Since the publication of his *Collected Poems* in 1978 he has published three more volumes of poetry.   [*viii*]